Early Occult Memory Systems of the Lower Midwest

ALSO BY B. H. FAIRCHILD

The Art of the Lathe

The Arrival of the Future

Local Knowledge

Such Holy Song: Music as Idea, Form, and Image in the Poetry of William Blake

Early

OCCULT MEMORY SYSTEMS

of

the Lower Midwest

B. H. FAIRCHILD

W. W. Norton & Company

New York London

Copyright © 2003 by B. H. Fairchild

For information about permission to reproduce selections from this
book, write to Permissions, W. W. Norton & Company, Inc.,
500 Fifth Avenue, New York, NY 10110

The text of this book is composed in Bulmer with the display set in
Matrix Narrow
Composition by Amanda Morrison
Manufacturing by The Courier Companies, Inc.
Book design by Blue Shoe Studio

Library of Congress Cataloging-in-Publication Data
Fairchild, B. H.
Early occult memory systems of the lower midwest / B. H. Fairchild.
p. cm.
ISBN 0-393-05096-3
1. Middle West—Poetry. I. Title.

PS3556.A3625 E26 2002
811'.54—dc21   2002071886

W. W. Norton & Company, Inc., 500 Fifth Avenue, New York, N.Y. 10110
www.wwnorton.com

W. W. Norton & Company Ltd., Castle House, 75/76 Wells Street,
London W1T 3QT

1 2 3 4 5 6 7 8 9 0

for all my people

Contents

Acknowledgments

I wish to thank the Kingsley Tufts Awards of the Claremont Graduate University, the Guggenheim Foundation, the Rockefeller Foundation, and California State University, San Bernardino, whose generous support gave me, for the first time in my life, a year's uninterrupted time to devote solely to writing. I also thank the MacDowell Arts Colony, the Bellagio Center, and the Frost Place, where many of these poems were written under the most ideal conditions that any poet could ask for. For recommendations, advice, or various kinds of support over the past three years, I am indebted to Ruth Burke, Louis Fernandez, Dana Gioia, R. S. Gwynn, Garrett Hongo, Laurel Lilienthal, Cleopatra Mathis, Robert Mezey, James Olney, Don Radke, Barry Sanders, Maurya Simon, Don Sheehan, Gerald Stern, Eri Yasuhara, and especially Anthony Hecht, without whose continuing encouragement, help, and example I would have walked away from the world of poetry some years ago. Grateful acknowledgment is also made to the following publications for poems which originally appeared in them (although, in some cases, in different form).

The American Scholar: "Delivering Eggs to the Girls' Dorm"
Café Review: "The Memory of a Possible Future"
DoubleTake: "The Potato Eaters"
The Hudson Review: "The Death of a Psychic," "On the Passing of Jesus Freaks from the College Classroom," "Two Scenes"
Image: "The Deposition," "The Problem"
The Mystic River Review: "Motion Sickness"

The New Yorker: "Early Occult Memory Systems of the Lower Midwest"

The Paris Review: "Holy Rollers, Snyder, Texas, 1951," "A Wall Map of Paris"

Solo: "History," "A Roman Grave"

The Sewanee Review: "At Omaha Beach," "Blood Rain," "At the Café de Flore," "The Second Annual *Wizard of Oz* Reunion"

The Southern Review: "The Big Bands: Liberal, Kansas, Summer of 1955," "The Blue Buick: A Narrative," "The Follies Burlesque, Market Street, Kansas City," "Mrs. Hill"

The Texas Review: "Brazil," "Luck"

TriQuarterly: "Rave On"

The Yale Review: "A Photograph of the *Titanic*"

"Mrs. Hill" was reprinted in *The Best American Poems of 2000,* ed. Rita Dove (New York: Scribner, 2000).

Early Occult Memory Systems of the Lower Midwest

On the rough wet grass of the backyard my father and mother have spread quilts. We all lie there, my mother, my father, my uncle, my aunt, and I too am lying there. First we were sitting up, then one of us lay down, and then we all lay down, on our stomachs, or on our sides, or on our backs, and they have kept on talking. They are not talking much, and the talk is quiet, of nothing in particular, of nothing at all in particular, of nothing at all. The stars are wide and alive, they seem each like a smile of great sweetness, and they seem very near. All my people are larger bodies than mine, quiet, with voices gentle and meaningless like the voices of sleeping birds. . . . By some chance, here they are, all on this earth; and who shall ever tell the sorrow of being on this earth, lying, on quilts, on the grass, in a summer evening, among the sounds of the night. May God bless my people, my uncle, my aunt, my mother, my good father, oh, remember them kindly in their time of trouble; and in the hour of their taking away.

After a little I am taken in and put to bed. Sleep, soft smiling, draws me unto her: and those receive me, who quietly treat me, as one familiar and well-beloved in that home: but will not, oh, will not, not now, not ever; but will not ever tell me who I am.

James Agee, *A Death in the Family*

PART ONE

Early Occult Memory Systems of the Lower Midwest

In his fifth year the son, deep in the backseat
of his father's Ford and the *mysterium*
of time, holds time in memory with words,
night, this night, on the way to a stalled rig south
of Kiowa Creek where the plains wind stacks
the skeletons of weeds on barbed-wire fences
and rattles the battered DeKalb sign to make
the child think of time in its passing, of death.

Cattle stare at flat-bed haulers gunning clumps
of black smoke and lugging damaged drill pipe
up the gullied, mud-hollowed road. *Road, this*
road. Roustabouts shouting from the crow's nest
float like Ascension angels on a ring of lights.
Chokecherries gouge the purpled sky, cloud-
swags running the moon under, and starlight
rains across the Ford's blue hood. *Blue, this blue.*

Later, where black flies haunt the mud tank,
the boy walks along the pipe rack dragging
a stick across the hollow ends to make a kind
of music, and the creek throbs with frog songs,
locusts, the rasp of tree limbs blown and scattered.
The great horse people, his father, these sounds,
these shapes saved from time's dark creek as the car
moves across the moving earth: *world, this world.*

Moses Yellowhorse Is Throwing Water Balloons from the Hotel Roosevelt

The combed lawn of the Villa Carlotta
cools the bare feet of my aesthetic friend
cooing *Beautiful, so beautiful, a dream* . . .
beneath the fat leaves of catalpa trees,
and my Marxist friend—ironic, mordant—
groans, *Ah, yes, indeed, how beautifully
the rich lie down upon the backs of the poor,*
but I am somewhere else, an empty field
near Black Bear Creek in western Oklahoma,
brought there by that ancient word, *dream,*
my father saying, *You had the dream, Horse,*
and two men toss a baseball back and forth
as the sun dissolves behind the pearl-gray strands
of a cirrus and the frayed, flaming branches
along the creek so that the men, too, seem
to be on fire, and the other one, a tall Pawnee
named Moses Yellowhorse, drops his glove,
But I wasn't a man there, and *there,* I know,
is Pittsburgh, and *man* means something more
like *human,* for as a boy I had heard
this story many times, beginning, always,
*He was the fastest I ever caught—the fastest,
I think, there ever was,* and I was stunned
because for a boy in America, to be the *fastest*

was to be a god, and now my father
and his brothers move behind a scrim
of dust in a fallow wheat field, a blanket
stretched between two posts to make a backstop,
a stand of maize to mark the outfield wall,
while their father watches, *If an Indian
can make it, then so by God can they*,
and so it goes, this story of failure
in America: Icarus unwarned,
strapped with his father's wings, my father
one winter morning patching the drive line
of an old Ford tractor with a strand
of baling wire, blood popping out along
his knuckles, and then in fury turning
to his father, *I'm not good enough,
I'll never get there, and I'm sorry,
I'm goddamned sorry*, while Moses Yellowhorse
is drunk again and throwing water balloons
from the Hotel Roosevelt because now
he is "Chief" Yellowhorse, and even though
in a feat of almost *angelic* beauty
he struck out Gehrig, Ruth, and Lazzeri
with nine straight heaters, something isn't right,
so one day he throws a headball at Ty Cobb,
then tells my father, *He was an Indian-hater,
even his teammates smiled*, and now, trying
to explain this to my friends, it occurs to me
that, unlike the Villa Carlotta, baseball is
a question of neither beauty nor politics

but rather mythology, the collective dream,
the old dream, of men becoming gods
or at the very least, as they remove
their wings, being recognized as men.

Mrs. Hill

I am so young that I am still in love
with Battle Creek, Michigan: decoder rings,
submarines powered by baking soda,
whistles that only dogs can hear. Actually,
not even them. Nobody can hear them.

Mrs. Hill from next door is hammering
on our front door shouting, and my father
in his black and gold gangster robe lets her in
trembling and bunched up like a rabbit in snow
pleading, *oh I'm so sorry, so sorry,*
so sorry, and clutching the neck of her gown
as if she wants to choke herself. *He said*
he was going to shoot me. He has a shotgun
and he said he was going to shoot me.

I have never heard of such a thing. A man
wanting to shoot his wife. His wife.
I am standing in the center of a room
barefoot on the cold linoleum, and a woman
is crying and being held and soothed
by my mother. Outside, through the open door
my father is holding a shotgun,
and his shadow envelops Mr. Hill,
who bows his head and sobs into his hands.

A line of shadows seems to be moving
across our white fence: hunched-over soldiers
on a death march, or kindly old ladies
in flower hats lugging grocery bags.

At Roman's Salvage tire tubes
are hanging from trees, where we threw them.
In the corner window of Beacon Hardware there's a sign:
WHO HAS 3 OR 4 ROOMS FOR ME. SPEAK NOW.
For some reason Mrs. Hill is wearing mittens.
Closed in a fist, they look like giant raisins.
In the *Encyclopaedia Britannica Junior*
the great Pharoahs are lying in their tombs,
the library of Alexandria is burning.
Somewhere in Cleveland or Kansas City
the Purple Heart my father refused in WWII
is sitting in a Muriel cigar box,
and every V-Day someone named Schwartz
or Jackson gets drunk and takes it out.

In the kitchen now Mrs. Hill is playing
gin rummy with my mother and laughing
in those long shrieks that women have
that make you think they are dying.

I walk into the front yard where moonlight
drips from the fenders of our Pontiac Chieftain.
I take out my dog whistle. Nothing moves.
No one can hear it. Dogs are asleep all over town.

The Potato Eaters

They are gathered there, as I recall, in the descending light
of Kansas autumn—the welder, the machinist, the foreman,
the apprentice—with their homemade dinners
in brown sacks lying before them on the broken rotary table.
The shop lights have not yet come on. The sun ruffling
the horizon of wheat fields lifts their gigantic shadows
up over the lathes that stand momentarily still and immense,

sleeping gray animals released from the turmoil,
the grind of iron and steel, these past two days.
There is something in the droop of the men's sleeves
and heavy underwater movements of their arms and hands
that suggests they are a dream and I am the dreamer,
even though I am there, too. I have just delivered the dinners
and wait in a pool of shadows, unsure of what to do next.

They unwrap the potatoes from the aluminum foil
with an odd delicacy, and I notice their still blackened hands
as they halve and butter them. The coffee sends up steam
like lathe smoke, and their bodies slowly relax
as they give themselves to the pleasure of the food
and the shop's strange silence after hours of noise,
the clang of iron and the burst and hiss of the cutting torch.

Without looking up, the machinist says something
to anyone who will listen, says it into the great cave

of the darkening shop, and I hear the words, *life,*
my life. I am a boy, so I do not know true weariness,
but I can sense what these words mean, these gestures,
when I stare at the half-eaten potatoes, the men,
the shadows that will pale and vanish as the lights come on.

Holy Rollers, Snyder, Texas, 1951

I.

Shades of brown: rust of the dirt road in
and the gulleys deepening to umber,
the taupe of winter grass along the shoulder,
the walls of the One True Gospel Church, dun,
with a plywood cross nailed above the door.
Nightmare fades to memory: the gray-brown hair
of Mrs. Hill pasted to her neck, the cracked
porcelain of her hands, her voice—*Rock*
of ages, cleft for me—cutting through the air
like a crow's cry. Beside her, Lester Hill
sits pale and mute with me, the awkward guest.
The preacher from the used car lot, dressed
in banker's clothes, shouts, *It's a hard road*
to heaven, Lord, but an easy ride to hell.
He wails, and the air thickens to a mud,
an agony, a swirl of groans and cries.
They find me later, curled into a ball,
humming *Rock of Ages* in a wheat field,
the brown earth of fear pressed against my eyes.

II.

In No Man's Land, standing on a rig deck
with my father, I watch two hawks begin

the long glide toward the east where wind-ripples
on a farm pond scatter light like gravel
or steel filings from a pail. When the drawworks
lunges into gear, the iron-plated deck shudders,
flattens to a monotone, and a grim rumble—
distant, monstrous, dark—comes thundering up
from five thousand feet below where rocks
and fossils older than the gods are ground
to dust and mud. I wipe the oil from my hand:
the earth below, the sky above, where a man
signals something from the crown block, arms
raised and holding in his hands the dying sun.

III.

A pipe seal somewhere makes a sobbing sound
the way, years later, in a London tavern
a hard man wept gladly that his grandson
had been found, and the women gathered near,
whispering what seemed psalms and prayers to him.

I walked out on the old stone bridge to see,
in the mirror of the Thames, my father, the rock
of ages, the sun above the crown block, and more:
the great river in its constant passage to the sea,
the dark truths that move across the ocean floor.

The Big Bands: Liberal, Kansas, Summer of 1955

I.

They were supposed to be dead, but they kept coming,
shunned by the cities but lunging into the gloom
of the outer counties, they kept moving along
two-lane highways on huge Greyhounds or night trains
destined for small towns without airports: Elk City,
Medicine Lodge, La Grange, Minneola, Meade, Cimarron.
After the year of troubles—the family business drowning
in red, the broken plates, black words, slammed doors,
my mother and father in separate rooms, the terrible silence
that grew like a clutch of weeds choking the little house—
after this, the summer came, the white skies, long evenings
unfolding like dark scarves tumbling to earth, mimosa blooms
floating from branches pummeled by baseballs in the side yard,
and they kept coming, the swing bands, the big bands,
those soft oceans of trombones and saxophones, of Les Brown,
Harry James, Kay Kaiser, Dorsey, and other priests
of music bound for Liberal, Kansas, in the summer of 1955.

II.

The green Packard I have just washed dries by the curb,
and the evening sun makes a bronze plunder
of brick streets. Cottonwood branches grown too low

loom and whisper. Cicadas begin to pulse, raucous
miracles, a chorus of things destined, of things
promised and given, while I wait on the front step
watching the sun melt and ooze over the car hood
until the bumper's chrome turns gold and the whole show
suggests Fred Astaire and Ginger Rogers gliding
through the front door to a dreamy trumpet fanfare.
They walk out smiling and awkward, my father
stiff in his brown suit, hand at my mother's elbow
as she, a woman I have never seen, leans
against him. As they step shyly toward the car,
a thick, warm sadness lifts from the grass, lifts
and pours over them in a kind of silver haze until
they seem luminous, El Greco-like. The street lamps
make shadows like black roses on the pavement.
My parents wave. The Packard rumbles and pulls away.

III.

I peek through a window of the Five-State Fair
Exhibition Hall and smile at the obsolete dance steps,
the surprise of elegance, a kind of embarrassed élan
and quaint formality from this man normally bent
over a machine lathe knee-deep in iron shavings,
this woman whose place was an ironing board or sink,
her hair pasted to neck and cheek. But now her hand
is delicate and light upon his shoulder, their modest
steps hardly visible, and behind them, a 16-piece

orchestra of boutonnieres and white dinner jackets
innocent as choral robes gleams in brass and silver,
and the blonde singer in what seems like a gesture
of worship embraces the air. This, in a building where
gigantic squash and cucumbers had been displayed
and where now my parents ease among a gathering
of farmers and roustabouts swathed in a gauze
of music, memorable as statues, in love again
with "Cherokee" and "Stardust" and "Mood Indigo."

IV.

It must have been this way before the war.
I think of my Uncle Harry dancing soft-shoe while
holding a gin-and-tonic in one hand and quoting lines
from *Double Indemnity*, my mother and her sisters
doing their Andrews Sisters imitation, my father
and uncles passing around a bottle of Southern Comfort
and swapping lies. It all comes back to me at midnight
as couples spill from the hall, clutching their
signed photographs of Sammy Kaye and Chris Connor,
their empty bottles of champagne saved as souvenirs.
And there, among the last to leave, are my parents
moving slowly, seeming lithe and moon-laden under
the field lights like celebrities stepping from flash bulbs
and limousines. I follow them along the gravel path
where the tree branches are loosening the starlight
and letting the lamps from the adjoining fairground

splash and litter the hoods of departing cars.
                                                    The last
to emerge are the musicians. They are much older
than I imagined. They are weary, lugging their horns
and flipping their last cigarettes like shooting stars
through the enveloping shadows. Their talk has a slow,
easy familiarity, the talk of old men on a long journey
accustomed to the ritual graces, the beginnings and endings,
of their trade, and they give themselves finally,
in single file, to the big bus rumbling at the edge of the lot,
then groaning into gear and slipping through the starlit night.

Hearing Parker the First Time

The blue notes spiraling up from the transistor radio
tuned to WNOE, New Orleans, lifted me out of bed
in Seward County, Kansas, where the plains wind riffed
telephone wires in tones less strange than the bird songs

of Charlie Parker. I played high school tenor sax the way,
I thought, Coleman Hawkins and Lester Young might have
if they were, like me, untalented and white, but *Ornithology*
came winding up from the dark delta of blues and dixieland

into my room on the treeless and hymn-ridden high plains
like a dust devil spinning me into the Eleusinian mysteries
of the jazz gods though later I would learn that his long
apprenticeship in Kansas City and an eremite's devotion

to the hard rule of craft gave him the hands that held
the reins of the white horse that carried him to New York
and 52nd Street, farther from wheat fields and dry creek beds
than I would ever travel, and then carried him away.

The Follies Burlesque, Market Street, Kansas City

The marquee flashed, THE ILLUMINATED RUNWAY OF JOY,
and the broadsides, brash and psychedelic
as Carmen Miranda's banana hats, flaunted
the large charms of Marie d'Amour, *ecdysiast*
extraordinaire, "direct from Paris and El Paso"
for at least two decades: platinum coiffure,
flaming lips, billowing breasts as generous
and pastoral as the foothills of northern New Mexico
or the swelling tides of Redondo Beach, a new frontier
for boys still bogged in the muddy ruts of late
adolescence, hungry for love and learning to nurse
3.2 beer from quart bottles. Inside, the lingering
odors of salt peanuts, sawdust soaking spilled beer
and who knows what from wood floors, and the sweat
of lonely men for whom the ragged thump and chime
of the snare and hi-hat were the death march of *eros*,
fibrillations in the heartbeat of love. The drummer
was ancient as stone and stoned as any bagged-out drunk
in the back rows or the crone who haunted the box office.
And those awful comics in clown shoes, flabby pants
and porkpie hats, with ladders to carry their case
to a higher court, whoopie cushions, and hip horns
raucous as Harpo Marx's. It was an opera house
with once gilded and velvet-cushioned balconies
now given to hoi polloi and slumming tourists
from the Hotel Muehlebach. Was anyone sober?

Did anyone buy those paper bags at intermission
stuffed with popcorn and porn: Popeye and Bluto
with hammers the size of Wyoming, Olive Oyl rich
with the sex secrets of the Orient? The second half
promised Lovely Lydia and the Dance that Made
Tijuana Blush, Jiminy Yiminy, Sir Satin
(the Sultan of Magic), and Natasha the Moscow Missile.
But there, third row center, behold the young poet
as Toulouse-Lautrec, chowing down on decadence
and Milk Duds, not short but short of breath, so unused
to cut-rate booze, the glitter of spangled G-strings
and those sequined propellers called tassels that he vaults
the aisle to boot in the filthiest restroom south of Chicago.

The next morning buying aspirin with trembling hands
at the corner Rexall, he sees in the back booth
a domestic scene from the brush of Norman Rockwell:
Marie d'Amour—hair in a snood, face pale as a nun's—
and Sir Satin over coffee and eggs. Between them
sits a child from the poet's childhood, the poet in fact,
dressed for Sunday School, all combed, ironed, and polished.
Drink your orange juice. Hurry. You'll be late.
Buttering the boy's toast, Sir Satin could be a bookkeeper
or carpet salesman too long on the job—bland,
gray at the temples, wool suit beginning to shine
at the shoulders. The poet stares: *They love him.*
I think they love each other. As the boy looks up,
a new sun is rising over Kansas City, over the Follies Burlesque,
the Hotel Muehlebach, the rumpled shadows of college boys

stumbling through its doors, over the winds that turneth ever, and lifting Market Street into an illuminated runway of joy.

Delivering Eggs to the Girls' Dorm

I am the egg man, . . .
John Lennon

For me it was the cherry blossoms flooding
Olive Street and softening the dawn,
the windows flung open in a yawn,
billowing curtains pregnant with the breeze,
the sounds of Procul Harum entering the air,
and fifty girls rising in their underwear.

O lost love. My girl and I had just split up.
The leaves of chestnut trees were rinsed in black,
the wind moaned grief, the moon was on the rack.
Humped over, stacking egg-crates in my Ford,
I was Charles Laughton ringing bells at Notre Dame—
spurned, wounded, but still in love with Sheila Baum.

Arriving at the gates of paradise,
I rang the service bell to wait on
Mrs. Cornish in her saintly apron
fumbling at the door, and the raucous gush
of female voices when she opened it. The flour
in her beard announced the darkness of the hour:

You're late. The hiss of bacon, pancake batter
as it kissed the grill, were a swarm of snakes to warn
the innocent away. Inside were virgins born,

like Sheila Baum, to stay that way. Outside
stood the egg man, despairing in his oval fate:
fifty girls staring, eggless, at an empty plate.

They may still be staring there. For emptiness
became my theme, sweeping eggshells
from my car, driving empty streets, fall's
cherry trees as bare as dormitory walls
washed by September rains. And the bells of Notre Dame
were as still as the broken shell of my dream of Sheila Baum.

Rave On

. . . wild to be wreckage forever.
James Dickey, "Cherrylog Road"

Rumbling over caliche with a busted muffler,
radio blasting Buddy Holly over Baptist wheat fields,
Travis screaming out *Prepare ye the way of the Lord*
at jackrabbits skittering beneath our headlights,
the Messiah coming to Kansas in a flat-head Ford
with bad plates, the whole high plains holding its breath,
night is fast upon us, lo, in these the days of our youth,
and we were hell to pay, or thought we were. Boredom
grows thick as maize in Kansas, heavy as drill pipe
littering the racks of oil rigs where in summer boys
roustabout or work on combine crews north as far
as Canada. The ones left back in town begin
to die, dragging main street shit-faced on 3.2 beer
and banging on the whorehouse door in Garden City
where the ancient madam laughed and turned us down
since we were only boys and she knew our fathers.
We sat out front spitting Red Man and scanned a landscape
flat as Dresden: me, Mike Luckinbill, Billy Heinz,
and Travis Doyle, who sang, *I'm gonna live fast,*
love hard, and die young. We had eaten all the life
there was in Seward County but hungry still, hauled ass
to old Arkalon, the ghost town on the Cimarron
that lay in half-shadow and a scattering of starlight,

and its stillness was a kind of death, the last breath
of whatever in our lives was ending. We had drunk there
and tossed our bottles at the walls and pissed great arcs
into the Kansas earth where the dust groweth hard
and the clods cleave fast together, yea, where night yawns
above the river in its long, dark dream, above
haggard branches of mesquite, chicken hawks scudding
into the tree line, and moon-glitter on caliche
like the silver plates of Coronado's treasure
buried all these years, but the absence of treasure,
absence of whatever would return the world
to the strangeness that as children we embraced
and recognized as *life. Rave on.*
                              Cars are cheap
at Roman's Salvage strewn along the fence out back
where cattle graze and chew rotting fabric from the seats.
Twenty bucks for spare parts and a night in the garage
could make them run as far as death and stupidity
required—on Johnson Road where two miles of low shoulders
and no fence line would take you up to sixty, say,
and when you flipped the wheel clockwise, you were there
rolling in the belly of the whale, belly of hell,
and your soul fainteth within you for we had seen it done
by big Ed Ravenscroft who said you would go in a boy
and come out a man, and so we headed back through town
where the marquee of the Plaza flashed CREATURE FROM
THE BLACK LAGOON in storefront windows and the Snack Shack
where we had spent our lives was shutting down and we
sang *rave on, it's a crazy feeling* out into the night

that loomed now like a darkened church, and sang loud
and louder still for we were sore afraid.
Coming up
out of the long tunnel of cottonwoods that opens onto
Johnson Road, Travis with his foot stuck deep into the *soul*
of that old Ford *come on, Bubba, come on* beating
the dash with his fist, hair flaming back in the wind
and eyes lit up by some fire in his head that I
had never seen, and Mike, iron Mike, sitting tall
in back with Billy, who would pick a fight with anything
that moved but now hunched over mumbling something
like a prayer, as the Ford lurched on spitting
and coughing but then smoothing out suddenly fast
and the fence line quitting so it was open field, then,
then, I think, we were butt-deep in regret and a rush
of remembering whatever we would leave behind—
Samantha Dobbins smelling like fresh laundry,
light from the movie spilling down her long blonde hair,
trout leaping all silver and pink from Black Bear Creek,
the hand of my mother, I confess, passing gentle
across my face at night when I was a child—oh, yes,
it was all good now and too late, too late, trees blurring
past and Travis wild, popping the wheel, oh too late
too late
and the waters pass over us the air thick
as mud slams against our chests though turning now
the car in its slow turning seems almost graceful
the frame in agony like some huge animal groaning
and when the wheels leave the ground the engine cuts loose

with a wail thin and ragged as a bandsaw cutting tin
and we are drowning breathless heads jammed against
our knees and it's a thick swirling purple nightmare
we cannot wake up from for the world is turning too
and I hear Billy screaming and then the whomp
sick crunch of glass and metal whomp *again back window*
popping loose and glass exploding someone crying out
tink tink of iron on iron overhead and then at last
it's over and the quiet comes
                           Oh so quiet. Somewhere
the creak and grind of a pumping unit. Crickets.
The tall grass sifting the wind in a mass of whispers
that I know I'll be hearing when I die. And so
we crawled trembling from doors and windows borne out
of rage and boredom into weed-choked fields barren
as Golgotha. Blood raked the side of Travis's face
grinning rapt, ecstatic, Mike's arm was hanging down
like a broken curtain rod, Billy kneeled, stunned,
listening as we all did to the rustling silence
and the spinning wheels in their sad, manic song
as the Ford's high beams hurled their crossed poles of light
forever out into the deep and future darkness. *Rave on.*

I survived. We all did. And then came the long surrender,
the long, slow drifting down like young hawks riding on
the purest, thinnest air, the very palm of God
holding them aloft so close to something hidden there,
and then the letting go, the fluttering descent, claws
spread wide against the world, and we become, at last,

our fathers. And do not know ourselves and therefore
no longer know each other. Mike Luckinbill ran a Texaco
in town for years. Billy Heinz survived a cruel divorce,
remarried, then took to drink. But finally last week
I found this house in Arizona where the brothers
take new names and keep a vow of silence and make
a quiet place for any weary, or lost, passenger
of earth whose unquiet life has brought him there,
and so, after vespers, I sat across the table
from men who had not surrendered to the world,
and one of them looked at me and looked into me,
and I am telling you there was *a fire in his head*
and his eyes were coming fast down a caliche road,
and I knew this man, and his name was Travis Doyle.

PART TWO

The Memory of a Possible Future

Images of something that has not yet happened and that may in fact never happen . . . are no different in nature from the images you hold of something that has already happened. They constitute the memory of a possible future rather than of the past that was.

Antonio R. Damasio, *Descartes' Error: Emotion, Reason, and the Human Brain*

Easy to recall, then, the sun
resurrected from its own ashes,
warmth swaddling the earth once more,
and then the long grip and slog up
from the original mud to who knows what
this time, but let's say an evolved race of saints
struggling through prayer and fasting
to achieve imperfection though it contradicts
their very nature, whose distaste
for copulation—with occasional lapses
resembling something like ballet or tai chi—
almost assures the survival of nature
and its trillions of ineffably beautiful
but useless life forms benefitting no one but themselves.

Less easy, the memory of the present,
of what is happening even as I speak
or do not speak, ensconced in this Italian villa
with plates of *fiche al cioccolato*
set before us by waiters in white coats,

and the purest lake, cradled by blue mountains
and attendant villages in delicate shades of ochre,
lapping at our cushioned feet. A *tableau vivant*
that all the while recedes—though held briefly
as we allow a rare Bordeaux to pool upon our tongues—
beneath scenes of my father as a boy
sleeping in an abandoned chicken house
and the small girl destined to bear me through a rage
of blood, sweat, and words that would soil
the fine linen I now lie down upon
(bearing with her, yes, my memory),
ripping from the hard Oklahoma earth
an endless burden of red-dirt potatoes
and vowing with each one never, *never* to forget.
Or what is happening now, oddly
and perhaps uniquely to me, as our host
reminds us that this *house* was once occupied
by German forces even as that same father now grown
lay down upon the beach at Tinian
and others, so many others, waited behind the gates
and were told that work would set them free.

And so, with a fine, and hopeless, desperation,
I try to imagine a *possible* past,
to *remember* a possible past, *with images*
no different in nature from the images
we have of something that has happened.
And of course it fails, memory fails,
as it always does, and the pale shadows

walk back into the gates of darkness,

the Gulag swells again with its unknown,

invisible, and unremembered millions,

the still unwritten words of Osip Mandelstam

are drawn backwards through his moving lips,

Arthur Smith bends between rows

of Georgia cotton, never to rise,

the Otoe who lived next door to my Grandfather's farm

climb down from their tall horses,

and Obed Theodore Swearingen himself

stands with a small boy in the shadows

of a cottonwood watching the unforgiving sun

fall once again—then, now, forever—into history.

Blood Rain

*Beset by an outbreak of plague in 1503, Nurembergers were
further terrified by a concurrent phenomenon called a blood rain,
. . . Dürer recorded the resulting stains on a servant girl's linen
shift: . . . a crucifix flanked by ghostly figures.*

Frances Russell, *The World of Dürer 1471–1528*

Like rust on iron, red algae invading rain.
And again, the plague. Nuremberg in ruin.
At home alone, the artist prays for grace
while, gates flung open, the neighbor's geese
roam the yard in droves, and their wild honks
and the ravings of a servant girl bring Dürer
to the window. She stands there, her wet hair
clumped in black strands, and her arms fall limp
in a great sob, her head lolling, while the damp
shift she wears blotters the rain in red streaks—
like wounds slowly spreading, Dürer sees, *to make
a sign*: in the bleeding fabric of her dress
as if etched in copper hangs Christ upon His Cross
between two ghosts. Cruel miracles, God's grace
drawn in God's blood on the body of a girl who sighs
at him, swoons, and collapses in the mud.

Outside, gutters turning scarlet, the dead
hauled from house to wagon, cries of women
battering the window panes. Inside, the burin
drops from Dürer's hand as the girl wakes

and rises from the bench below his portrait,
done in Munich the year of the apocalypse, but
never to be sold, never to leave the artist's house.
She touches once more God's message on her dress,
then turns and stares at the painting's face
so solemn, so god-like in its limpid gaze,
that she backs away to study the long brown locks
spread evenly about His shoulders, the beatific
right hand held more gently than the blessing
of a priest, and the inscription in a tongue
she does not understand. *This is Christ!*
No, it's me, he says, touching hand to chest,

the rough right hand, the human chest, the heart's dream
of art's divinity as death rolls down the street.

The Death of a Psychic

The obituary in the *L.A. Times* says that you foresaw
your own death, also a boy, dead, in a storm drain
with the wrong shoes on the wrong feet. Death
became your specialty: a yellow shirt, the flung

corsage near, vaguely, water, the odd detail drawing
squad cars and ambulance to the scene you dreaded.
I imagine nightmares that you woke up to instead
of from, the heavy winter coat of prophecy that hung

from your shoulders any season, especially summer
when mayhem bloomed below a bleeding sun
and dark angels, gorged on smog and heat, unfurled
their wings to wake you gasping in your dampened bed,

again, once more. No theophanies, no "still small voice"
or hovering dove, but only gray, murky hunches
bubbling from the mud of intuition, the sudden starts
and flights of vision, and of course, its shadow, fear.

But to live haunted by the knowledge of a certain year
when you would stumble in your flannel houserobe
through a sunlit kitchen and lie down on cold linoleum
beneath, at last, the wide wings of the present tense.

History

Wired tight on No Doz and coffee, I've cut iron
for two straight days and nights, and the white cowbird
drifting down the sun blurs through my rankled eyes
and the grease-smeared windows above my lathe. There,
toward the vanishing point where the cowbird dips
and hovers, is history: a ghost town, the least of all
lost civilizations. Beer City, my grandmother said,
was the Sodom and Gomorrah of the plains, where the whores
worked above the Yellow Snake Saloon and rode the wagons
through No Man's Land each morning to Liberal, Kansas,

where they could sleep in safety. And the next evening,
back through two thousand head of cattle ranging along
Kiowa Creek the whores rode in their flouncy dresses
and broad-brimmed hats fluttering in the dusty wind, rode
to what? The fierce eyes and mouths of men who held
them with hands like rope, who might have been horses
for all their heavy silences and rank smells that not even
a long boiling bath could cure. One time the madam
shot Bill Smith, the self-appointed sheriff, for rustling
her cows, and the town joined in, blasting his corpse

like a burlap bag through the gray mud of Main Street.
The only law in No Man's Land, my grandmother said, was
that the big ones ate the little ones. But with luck a whore
might marry one of these men who, with luck, might rustle

enough cattle to start a herd that, surviving drought,
dust storm, and blizzard, might grow into a ranch, and then,
then, they would bring the Law to No Man's Land because, after all,
you can't keep a herd without it, what with all the rustlers
around, and *that*, my difficult and honorable grandmother
told me one night late when the plains wind whined against

the tin siding, *that is history*. Outside, the rack
is full, the brown land beyond broken only by a rig
whose drill collars I'm turning, and I think of a flood
of buffalo over the land the way it looked before they
were all killed off because buffalo hide made cheap conveyor
belts for shops back East like the one I'm working in now.
History, I think, is that cowbird perched on the far end
of the rack who waits for the shop doors to shut, waits
for a moaning, red mob of cows to stir and start again
the long walk north, as I begin the long walk back to town.

The Decline of Utopian Ideas in the West

for Paul

The old roughnecks between jobs drunk in their cars outside the
bowling alley; the schoolteacher in her rented room in love with
the mechanic and dreaming of moving to Houston: new front tires
for the Dodge, bright yellow curtains for the kitchen windows, a
TV; the blood sunset in the corners of my father's eyes after he
worked a lathe for two days and nights; 3 a.m., the welder on No
Doz and Benzedrine smoking his last Pall Mall, listening to
Tammy Wynette, waiting for the driller to show; the way the
dust would bronze the window ledges and the kitchen table, a dust
devil spinning a trash can in the backyard; the dog house at
the rig, the Goodyear calendar with a big-breasted nude blonde
kneeling in a truck tire, the empty bottle of Jim Beam, roustabouts
passed out on cots; the little bridge that pain walked between
astonishment and horror when John Santos caught his hand in
the pipe clamps, his eyes dull as glass marbles afterwards; my
mother enrolling me in school in the little boom town, *oh, you're
one of those*; a necklace of teardrop trailers on the edge of town,
Lester Hill lived in one and went to holy roller meetings with his
mom and had nightmares; the brown teeth of the trailer kids;
revival meetings at the football field on Sunday afternoons, Gimpy
Neiderland saved from booze for the fourth time; the bankers
strolling out of the Petroleum Club cleaning their teeth with
toothpicks and loosening their belts; the old men in the back room
of the pool hall, the click of dominoes, amber beer bottles glowing

in the late afternoon sun; the boy with green hair and lipstick who hung around the alley; Tommy Johnson, the old ex-Wobbly who hauled mud for the Lacey brothers, skull crushed from a dropped drill collar; his wife, Luanne, who worked the ticket booth at the theater, got drunk one night and lay down on the railroad tracks; the wildcatter walking into the bank with the bad news, noticing for the first time the plush carpet, the gleam of polished mahogany, the fragrance of orange peels rising from the hands of the receptionist; oilfield kids standing in line at the El Dorado Theatre in Snyder to see *King Solomon's Mines*; my mother listening to Billie Holiday and staring at a photograph of my father; my father with his head in bandages as I cradle in my palm the steel burr they removed from his eye; Lester and I walking the dirt road behind his trailer, reciting once again the oath of the Green Lantern: *In brightest day, in blackest night, no evil shall escape my sight.*

Luck

for Don Radke

I sit looking into the mirror at the bitter man
sitting opposite me whose book has been rejected
for the last time: the familiar face I have never liked,
the mournful eyes, mournful even in happiness,
broken mouth, nose like a fig, the melancholy face
of a man whose gift of perseverance I have admired
though now he disappoints me as I watch
the blue bile of self-pity welling up in drab,
sad little lunettes below his eyes. I begin to think,
I am lucky, I am lucky, to live in a country
where the son of a machinist can piss away his time
writing poems, . . . and I think of that odd word,
lucky, its strange sound, the "uck" sound
of a duck barfing or even choking to death,
its ridiculous webbed feet fanning the air,
writhing *uck, uck,* or the miserable, queer sound
of galoshes unstuck from the mud, *uck*, the sound
of disgust at the vile, sick, nasty, repugnant,
the blackened lemon stuck under the fruit bin, *uck*,
the gross, the foul, the *lucky*, rhyming with FUCK E
as in Fuck Everett written in dust on the back
of a semi hauling dog food to Peoria or painted
in Day-Glo on the water tower by E's acne-ridden,
rabid ex-girlfriend, but there is, on the other hand,

lucky's lovely "l" sound, preferred by Yeats
among all phonemes, called a *liquid* and cited
in all the Intro. to Poetry texts for its melody,
its grace, its small-breasted, skinny-hipped, lithe
evocativeness, "l," the Audrey Hepburn of consonants,
as in lily, ladle, lap, lip, lust, labia, loquacious,
or LUCKY!, e.g., *Hail! Good fortune attend thee,*
Horatio, you lucky bastard, or *Good luck, Leonard,*
I hope you get lucky, or the word being implicit
in the deed, therefore the very act, the event, of luck,
the sun coming out in the fifth inning, a ten-dollar bill
falling out of the dryer, the tragic diagnosis reversed,
Jules and Jim and *One-Eyed Jacks* back-to-back,
no school, a cool summer, a warm winter, the big,
beautiful book containing twenty years of poems
WITH YOUR NAME ON THEM, *lucky*, a stupid word,
a wrong word, easily used, badly understood, the tiny,
pathetic wet dream of me and Everett and that whole town
surrounding a water tower where a girl stands
with phosphorescent green paint dribbling down
her wrist, mumbling, *luck, oh luck, just a little, just some, luck.*

A Roman Grave

He begins to fear the gray morning light,
the absence out of which each day arises,
an iron sun dragging through a grinding fog.

Along the mews the long cars of the Romanovs
move quietly as clouds to line the curb
of the Russian Orthodox Church in Exile.

He sees them far below as crows, black umbrellas
slick with rain beneath the red-leaved trees,
old women draped in veils and funeral scarves.

A Europe of confusions, history's scattered
flocks mumbling unintelligible prayers
while the chauffeurs take out their cigarettes.

Later, he watches diggers on the Thames'
south side haul up rocks from a Roman grave,
a girl buried beside her brother. Strata

lie piled like quilts beside the small pits
where a man and woman kneel in their shadows.
The dead in their stone sleep are roused into

history. The living pray into the earth and wait.

On the Passing of Jesus Freaks from the College Classroom

They seemed to come in armies, whole platoons
uniformed in headbands, cut-off jeans,
butt-long hair that fell down in festoons,
and their grins were the ends that justified the means.

But one was different. And alone. His wrist tattoo
cried FATHER on a severed heart that bled.
His arms hung limp as vines, his nails were blue,
his silence was the chorus of the dead.

"Are you saved?" they asked. "Saved from what," I said.
"The flames of hell, your rotten, sinful past,
your thing for Desdemona," for we had read
the tragedies, and *Othello* was the last.

"What's Iago's motive? Was he just *sinful*?"
They thought they knew but waited for a hint.
He raised his hands and wept, "Evil, fucking Evil."
And he meant it. *And he knew what he meant.*

Brazil

This is for Elton Wayne Showalter, redneck surrealist
who, drunk, one Friday night tried to hold up the local 7-Eleven
with a caulking gun, and who, when Melinda Bozell boasted
that she would never let a boy touch her "down there," said,
"Down there? You mean, like, Brazil?"

                    Oh, Elton Wayne,
with your silver-toed turquoise-on-black boots and Ford Fairlane
dragging, in a ribbon of sparks, its tailpipe down Main Street
Saturday nights, you dreamed of Brazil and other verdant lands,
but the southern hemisphere remained for all those desert years
a vast mirage shimmering on the horizon of what one might call
your mind, following that one ugly night at the Snack Shack
when, drunk again, you peed on your steaming radiator
to cool it down and awoke at the hospital, groin empurpled
from electric shock and your pathetic maleness swollen
like a bruised tomato. You dumb bastard, betting a week's wages
on the trifecta at Raton, then in ecstasy tossing the winning ticket
into the air and watching it float on an ascending breeze
with the lightness and supple dip and rise of a Bach passacaglia
out over the New Mexico landscape forever and beyond: gone.
The tears came down, but the spirit rose late on Sunday night
on a stepladder knocking the middle letters from FREEMAN GLASS
to announce unlimited sexual opportunities in purple neon
for all your friends driving Kansas Avenue as we did each night
lonely and boredom-racked and hungering for someone like you,
Elton Wayne, brilliantly at war in that flat, treeless county

against maturity, right-thinking, and indeed intelligence
in all its bland, local guises, so that now reading the announcement
in the hometown paper of your late marriage to Melinda Bozell
with a brief honeymoon at the Best Western in Junction City,
I know that you have finally arrived, in Brazil, and the Kansas
that surrounds you is an endless sea of possibility, genius, love.

Weather Report

We will have a continuation of today tomorrow.

Clouds will form those ragged gloves
in which the hands of God make giant fists
as He grits His teeth against the slaves
of time. And the sun and moon will never rest

from the boring grind of dark and light:
subway tokens glittering the ground,
dogs in their habits, the hours soon or late,
nuns and assassins in their daily round.

The divorcée coming from the laundromat
knows the cycles of laundry and despair:
back then, the towels they shared, but now a basket
filled with someone else's underwear.

Eichmann lies in bed and reads a novel;
a Holocaust survivor sets himself on fire.
The thief's in church, the priest is in the brothel;
the sky is clear, the weatherman's a liar.

God shakes His fists eternally to say,
we're having more of yesterday today.

The Second Annual *Wizard of Oz* Reunion in Liberal, Kansas

They have come once more, the small ones.
They crowd around my mother and her friends
at the F. Nightingale Retirement Home
and sing *Wizard of Oz* songs like hymns

and let themselves be called "munchkins"
by the palsied, ancient ones who cling
to that memory and Dorothy taken
through the Kansas air but cannot recall

the green city or the yellow road that leads there.
Mrs. Beaudry, who owned the coffee shop,
cannot find her hands, and Mr. MacIntyre
is searching for his long-dead wife and is happy,

finally, when she calls. For these the actors
sing their tunes, and for the wheelchair aged
and the ones on metal walkers that clump
like awkward giants through the halls.

For these the rayon flowers, and the Bible
opened to a text they cannot read. For these
a trip to Oz Land, and a photo sent
with a letter in which my mother writes,

Some children came today. They seemed so grown
and fine and reminded me of you back when.
This, to a man with neither courage, brain,
nor heart to find his way back home again.

The Welder, Visited by the Angel of Mercy

Something strange is the soul on the earth.
Georg Trakl

Spilled melons rotting on the highway's shoulder sweeten
the air, their bruised rinds silvering under the half-moon.
A blown tire makes the pickup list into the shoulder
like a swamped boat, and the trailer that was torn loose

has a twisted tongue and hitch that he has cut away,
trimmed, and wants to weld back on. Beyond lie fields
of short grass where cattle moan and drift like clouds, hunks
of dark looming behind barbed wire. The welder, crooning

along with a Patsy Cline tune from the truck's radio,
smokes his third joint, and a cracked bottle of Haig and Haig
glitters among the weeds, the rank and swollen melons.
Back at St. Benedict's they're studying Augustine now,

the great rake in his moment sobbing beneath the fig trees,
the child somewhere singing, take and read, take and read.
What they are not doing is fucking around in a ditch
on the road to El Paso ass-deep in mush melons

and a lame pickup packed with books that are scattered now
from hell to breakfast. Jesus. Flipping the black mask up,
he reaches into the can for a fresh rod, clamps it,
then stares into the evening sky. Stars. The blackened moon.

The red dust of the city at night. Roy Garcia,
a man in a landscape, tries to weld his truck and his life
back together, but forgetting to drop the mask back down,
he touches rod to iron, and the arc's flash hammers

his eyes as he stumbles, blind, among the fruit of the earth.
The flame raging through his brain spreads its scorched wings
in a dazzle of embers, lowering the welder, the good student,
into his grass bed, where the world lies down to sleep

until it wakes once more into the dream of Being:
Roy and Maria at breakfast, white cups of black coffee,
fresh melons in blue bowls, the books in leather bindings
standing like silent children along the western wall.

PART THREE

The Blue Buick: A Narrative

*I read the Classics in an English edition; but I would also relax
by unrolling a map of the sky on a big table and covering each
constellation with precious stones from our coffers, marking the
largest stars with the most beautiful diamonds, finishing out
these designs with the most colorful gems, filling the spaces
between with a stream of the most beautiful pearls from Léouba's
collection, . . . They were all beautiful! And I recited to myself that
immortal, and for me unforgettable, page by Marbode on the sym-
bolism of precious stones which I had just discovered in* Le Latin
mystique *by Rémy de Gourmont, a gem of a book, a compilation,
a translation, an anthology, which turned me upside-down and,
in short, baptized me, or at the very least, converted me to Poetry,
initiated me into the Word, catechized me.*

Blaise Cendrars, "La chambre noir de l'imagination," in *Le
Lotissement du ciel*

*My imagination goes some years backward, and I remember a
beautiful young girl singing at the edge of the sea in Normandy
words and music of her own composition. She thought herself
alone, stood barefooted between sea and sand; sang with lifted
head of the civilizations that there had come and gone, ending
every verse with the cry:*
    "O Lord, let something remain"

William Butler Yeats, *A Vision*

A boy standing on a rig deck looks across the plains.

A woman walks from a trailer to watch the setting sun.

A man stands beside a lathe, lighting a cigar.

Imagined or remembered, a girl in Normandy

sings across a sea, *that something may remain:*

A blue Buick Dynaflow, sleek, fat, grand, useless
for dragging Main, gunning off the stoplight sluggish
as a cow, but on the highway light and smooth as flight,
the Louvre's Winged Samothrace that Roy kept
a postcard of above his lathe, for he had been
to Paris, where he first met his wife, Maria.
I knew them those last years in Kansas before
they left for California, from the summer
of the last great dust storm when I crawled home from school
because I could not see the sidewalk beneath my feet,
the silence hanging, too, in air, the whole town drowning
under dust like Pompeii or Herculaneum,
and I imagined its history now left to me,
and I could tell, then, of the loneliness that fell
across the plains, across the town, looking out
on bald horizons undisturbed by tree lines,
and the blue-gray steel of winter sky brutal
in its placid, constant stare, like the hit man
in *Macbeth, let it come down*, and if there is an Eye
of God, the seer and the seen, it is that sky:
vast, merciless, and bored. Too bored to tell again
the old story of housewives gone mad, farmers standing
alone by the back fence of the back forty weeping
in desperation, the Mexican girl walking nude
out of a wheat field and offering herself
to an entire rig crew for a dollar each, boys
outside the Cottonwood Club beating each other
unconscious for nothing better to do . . .

The music: an old Reinhardt and Grappelli record
that Roy and Maria brought from Paris,
the sweet, frail voice of an unknown woman
singing *Don't Worry 'Bout Me*. It hovers over
and around them, aurora-like, the frayed light
of a blanched photograph, it pursues them always
and everywhere, sailing down Highway 54
in that big boat under a star-strewn sky, parked
under cottonwoods along the Cimarron River,
watching a late-game home run lift into the lights,
and it was there full-volume when Roy came home
from work and they began to dance, martinis in hand,
and soon you were there in the Hot Club in Paris
rather than a tiny Airstream trailer parked
along the southern outskirts of Liberal, Kansas,
where a boy, amazed, sat at a yellow formica
breakfast table watching something that might be,
he wondered, some form, some rare, lucky version,
of human happiness.
                    Happiness. And surely
it was there from the beginning, she a dancer,
he a Rotary scholar from Texas escaping Cambridge
to join the excitement of Paris in the early fifties
where he knew Baldwin, even the old man Cendrars,
hung out at jazz clubs along Boulevard St. Germain,
and wrote for two years before returning home
and a season with the Class A Lubbock Hubbers.
After that, seven failed years in Hollywood
(failed, though he would quote with pride the lines he wrote

for Trumbo's *Lonely Are the Brave*), then vanishing
in the oil fields of Bakersfield, trying still to write,
lugging a trailer full of books and landing, finally,
in southwest Kansas in a machine shop managed
by my father, where Roy believed that he was
on the *edge* of something, something *rare*, something more,
even, than Paris, though to my mind it was just
the northern edge of the Oklahoma Panhandle,
known as No Man's Land in the days when horse thieves
and rustlers called it home, and what Roy found there
I still try to understand. Absence. Mystery.
Roy worshiped it, called it *negative capability*
and quoted Keats, said in poetry and lathework,
both arts of precision, it was what lay beyond
the *mot juste*, the closest tolerance, the finest cut,
it was where it all, finally, ended.

                                    Roy Garcia
was the only man my father hired again
after he showed up drunk. *Because he's brilliant,
the best machinist I've ever seen*, and he had seen
a few. *And he's an educated man*, he said,
with that distant, almost spiritual admiration
of someone who had never finished high school.
And he has a good excuse. He meant of course
the seizures, which came on rarely but each time
seemed to happen twice, for Roy would turn to drink—
out of shame, Maria said—and he could handle
one drink, maybe two, but the drunkenness brought on
by shame—not immediate, but lingering, a sense

of being doomed or damned, as if he blamed himself—
would cause another seizure, and Maria
and my father would have to treat him like a child:
confine him to his trailer, put him back on
Tegretol, and make him pull himself together
before he came back on the job. But with "good excuse,"
I knew my father, too, was thinking of his brother,
Mike, who had the same disease. And so he made me
Roy's apprentice, to learn from him but also
to look out for him. Roy could tell when one
was coming on—a void, a tension, in his stomach—
and would lie down on the wooden ramp beside his lathe,
and I would shout for help, someone to keep him
from swallowing his tongue. The *shame* of it, she said,
but if there was shame, there was the other thing as well,
the brief spell before the fit came on that made it
all, he said, almost worthwhile: the rush of light,
his body looking down upon his other body.
At college later, reading Brutus's line, *Hath he
not the falling-sickness*, I would think of this
and wonder: the going hence, the coming hither,
all of it, a confusion and a mystery in those days.

From Roy's Journal: *The marriage of heaven and hell. If the aura
is a state of grace, then what is the seizure? If in the aura I lose my
body, what do I lose in the other? The old woman on the steps of St.
Eustache weeping, terrified that she had lost her soul.*

About one thing, though, I can be exact: that Buick,
baby blue with a white ragtop, double-wide
white sidewalls and about two tons of chrome grillwork
navigating Main Street all fat-assed, gas-guzzling,
and anti-environmental as they come. A dream,
I thought, a big blue dream that summer driving back
from Amarillo with my girl nuzzling against me
and Roy and Maria in the backseat singing
Crazy or *I Fall to Pieces* into the stars,
and sometimes on a familiar stretch of blacktop
with no curves or dips and a moon to light the way,
the cathedral dome of night sky turned upside-down
in the blue laminations of the hood, I would
turn off the headlights for a while and fly miles
and miles from earth, more alone and yet not alone
than I have ever been, and just as we reached home,
crossing No Man's Land, the rim of the world would begin
to blaze, and with the rising sun we would drift slowly
back to earth, back to Kansas.
                                        Since Paris, Roy
and Maria had been apart just once, when he ran off
to Bakersfield and she chose to stay behind, working
in L.A. with Bronislava Nijinska at her studio
in Hollywood, trying hard to breathe new life
into a ballet career that had never grown beyond
the corps of the smallest company in Paris.
Nijinska finally, of course, with a sense of guilt
almost maternal had to make Maria face
reality, but oddly—since they had grown so close,

because Maria was, as Nijinska often said,
the very echo of her famous protégée,
Maria Tallchief, because it was that tragic case
of desire, self-sacrifice, and even talent
devoured by the accident of failure—gave her
the Buick, a gift from a rich patron, as a kind
of tacit consolation. Seeing this as a sign
and wonder—the end of one life, the beginning
of another—Maria then drove straight to Roy
in Bakersfield, and they had been together
ever since. In her L.A. days, while Roy
was reviving dying screenplays, Maria—
like most dancers, I suppose—also dreamed of acting,
and sometimes we would drive to old Arkalon,
the ghost town on the Cimarron, and there among
the ruins, broken walls, and traces of foundations,
while we drank Pearl beer from quart bottles and gazed
at scraps of night sky sliding down the contours
of the car, she recited lines from parts that she
had *almost* won: Blanche Dubois, or Laura
from *Glass Menagerie*, and Roy would lean back
and look up into the trees and dark beyond, watching
smoke from his cigar rise like small dirigibles
that bore the words of a once aspiring actress
and almost famous dancer named Maria Patterson.

What did I know? I was a blank slate—a phrase,
by the way, I only learned from Roy (read Locke,
then Blake)—and all I knew is that I had to *know*.

To know, in a town with a one-room storefront
library where Durant's *The Story of Philosophy*
was the raft I was floating on, though slowly sinking,
too, in an endless cycle of work/eat/sleep, haunting
the only bookstore within two hundred miles
in Amarillo, when I could get there, and watching
cars pass through to exotic California
with those bright orange plates that seemed to say, *life*
is somewhere else. Sometimes I would drive aimlessly
through No Man's Land, and if I stopped at a little town
called Slapout and asked the lady at the Quick Stop
for the population, she would say, *Seven,*
but the eighth is on its way, and point to her belly.
For God's sake.

            There were, on the other hand, the movies.
I remember one, especially: *The Country Girl.*
Grace Kelly played the wife of an ex-Broadway star,
an aging alcoholic who's been out of work
but straight for years. The director, William Holden,
needs him badly for his new play, and when he visits
their little drab apartment, Kelly talks across
an ironing board where clothes are piled, her graying hair
lies lank and damp against her neck, but books fill the room,
and Holden picks one up: *Montaigne, I find him*
too polite. Wonderful, I thought, stupidly,
but then Holden understands, these books are *hers*,
and he begins to see that she's the strong one here,
the wise one, she's the one to pull her husband up.
And I saw it, too, or rather saw Grace Kelly,
golden, rising like Athena in a field of books

to make her husband rise, reborn, as an actor
once again, and of course Holden falls in love with her,
but she in turn then falls in love with the new man
she has half-created and *everyone gets exactly
what they deserve*, and walking home that evening
with a half-moon lifting over the machine shop
where I had just spent one more day, I thought
in my pathetic, redneck way, *That must be what folks
call "art."*

   Art. What did I know? Nothing, until
Roy and Maria came to town. *Enough Grappelli,*
she would say, and put on a symphony, Mozart,
maybe, or Dvorak's *New World,* which made me
swallow hard and turn my face away because, well,
it was *beautiful*, a word I wasn't easy with back then,
and because, I know now, it seemed to be about the plains
which in their endless silence had no music until
that moment, when I saw my father, his four brothers,
a scrabble farm and three-room house against an empty
landscape and barren future. Sometimes, returning from
a drive to nowhere in particular, she sang fragments
of *Caro nome,* and I would think, how strange,
a song like that here, now, among grazing cattle,
barbed wire, mesquite, endless rows of maize,
and pumping units bobbing up and down like insane,
gigantic blackbirds. And stranger still, Roy
might speak grandly into the wind and waiting fields:
  *In my craft or sullen art,
  Exercised in the still night
  When only the moon rages*

And lovers lie abed
With all their griefs in their arms . . .
or Keats or Shakespeare or the new one by Lowell
he loved, "The Fat Man in the Mirror," from Werfel:
Only a fat man with his beaver on his eye
Only a fat man,
Only a fat man
Bursts the mirror. O, it is not I!
which I never understood, though I do now,
perhaps. So they were teachers, I suppose, though
messengers is more the word, messengers, travelers
from another world—as Eluard said, the world
that is inside this one—and they came bearing
the messages, the anthology, that would change
my life: St. Augustine's *Confessions*, *The Brothers
Karamazov*, Conrad, *A Little Treasury
of Modern Poetry*, Gombrich's survey, Hart Crane,
Dickinson's *Collected*, Ring Lardner, Salinger,
Flannery O'Connor, a Chekhov story called
"The Student," *Winesburg, Ohio*, Joyce's "The Dead,"
a little book on Kierkegaard by Auden, "The Snows
of Kilimanjaro," a signed copy of Baldwin's
Go Tell It on the Mountain, and what must have been
a first edition of *Let Us Now Praise Famous Men*.
But at the end of the bottom shelf of books that lined
their little trailer was one in French by Blaise Cendrars:
Le Lotissement du Ciel (*The Subdividing
of the Sky*, my translation), the strangest book,
Roy said, he ever read by the most intriguing man

he ever knew. Cendrars, the one-armed legend,
veteran of the front in both world wars, citizen
of a dozen countries, friend of Chagall, Léger,
Apollinaire, Modigliani: a man who had read
everything, done everything, and when Roy
knew him still talked endlessly of *Sky*'s main subject:
the levitation of saints in the ecstatic state
called by St. John of the Cross *al arrobamiento
de amor*: the ravishment of love. *Cendrars,
the old surrealist*, Roy would say, *obsessesed
with bodies rising in air when his only son,
the pilot, died by falling to earth.* He came back
to this repeatedly. And to Giordano Bruno,
who Roy said was more important than Galileo,
and he taught me Bruno's memory system,
the nearest thing to immortality, he said,
for then I would forget nothing, and everything
would be imprinted on my soul.

The Journal: *Cendrars in "The Ravishment of Love." "The saint
also has his migraines and his gross lassitude. . . . He is suspicious
of illusions, dream-somnambulism, the acrobatics of certain drunk
and manic states, and the nervous breakdowns of certain epileptics
and neurotics."*

So I remembered
everything, the small as well as large, the photo
of Roy and Robert Rossen in Hollywood
(the manuscript of *Treasure of the Sierra Madre*

69

with Rossen's name on it), all the stories
that Maria told of Nijinska and her brother,
the trip to Amarillo when Patsy Cline performed,
even the hometown ball games we would go to,
we three on summer evenings when the fragrance
of new mown outfield grass was hanging in the air
and the lights came on to carve the darkening sky
into a big blue bowl. *A ball diamond*, he would say,
is the most aesthetically pure form ever given
to a playing field, and as a student of geometry
I could understand that, the way the diamond fits
inside a circle enclosed within a larger one
extending from the arc along the outfield wall.
And the way the game itself falls into curves:
runners rounding base paths; the arc of the long ball's
sudden rise and floating, slow descent, sometimes
into the outer darkness beyond the left-field wall;
the shape a double play can take when the shortstop
snags the ball on his far right and the second baseman
makes a fluid pivot so the ball seems to glide
in an unbroken line around to first; and of course
a killer curve or good knuckle ball by someone like
Preacher Roe or Whitey Ford whose looping arc
briefly mesmerizes the batter it deceives;
all a game of curves and arcs, though Maria
said it was a game of tension, a gathering,
then release, a kind of sexual tension, the way
the pitcher coiled, then unwound, and of course
the explosive letting go, and she said it in a way

that made me stop and think awhile. In a plane once
I saw a diamond far below all lit up,
an emerald resting on the breast of darkness, and now
I recall Maria and the curve from her neck along
the jawline to her raised chin as she followed
the arc of the ball in flight and the way her eyes
gave back the flare of the outfield lights at night.

As with baseball and poetry, so with lathework,
arts of precision: an able catcher sets his feet
to avoid the extra step that makes him miss
the steal at second, a poet hears the syllable
before the word, a good machinist "feels" the cut
before he measures it. These minute distinctions
were Roy's delight, *The Machinist's Handbook*
his guide to prosody. And I tried but somehow
failed the craft—in fact, one time almost ran the bit
into the chuck, unknown to my worried father,
who was losing hope for me: if Roy couldn't teach me,
who could? But my head was in baseball, books, music:
my tenor saxophone and I would someday be
on 52nd Street in New York, where we belonged,
and so I made Roy talk about his father's friend,
the great jazz trumpeter, Roy Eldridge, whose name
he took, and the jazz scene in Paris in the fifties
where Roy and Maria on any given night
could hear Bud Powell, Lester Young, Kenny Clarke,
Dexter Gordon, even Sidney Bechet, even sometimes
the Bird himself, and Maria, smiling, recalled

standing outside The Ringside, later The Blue Note,
one night as Parker's astonishing long riff
on "Green Dolphin Street" rose over the waiting crowd,
over the lamps reflected in the Seine, up and beyond
Hausmann's Paris and the opulent Palais Garnier,
a black man's music rising and hovering over
this pearl of Europe from a small room far below
on the Rue d'Artois.

          Decades later I would walk
this street and others: Rue Coquilliere,
where Roy met Cendrars, where, I imagined,
he rose finally from the table, feeling the weight,
the burden, of being young and unknown, and strolled
past Saint Eustache through the jazz-thick air of the clubs
in Les Halles to the little room on Rue du Jour
that he shared with Maria, where they drank the last
of their wine and gazed from the balcony toward
the distant future. And whatever they saw there,
it could not have been Liberal, Kansas. What dreams
they must have had! Raising his glass of Cointreau
after dinner, Roy would speak the magic words
of Baudelaire, *Je suis comme le roi d'un pays pluvieux*,
and Maria would pull the album from the hope chest
and turn to the photographs, so predictable
they broke your heart: a girl and boy leaning
against the stones of Pont Neuf, the Seine stretching
behind them, the girl small, sharp-boned, bright brown eyes,
a dancer's bun, and you could almost see her thin lips
trembling with the hesitation that sometimes precedes

pure joy, the boy with slicked-back hair, cigarette
dangling from one hand, the other pressing his girl close.
That evening, I remember, Maria was playing
an old 78 of Bidu Sayao singing Massenet,
and for a moment in my eyes they froze, Maria
lost in thought, staring down into the images
as if she wanted to walk into them, Roy
gazing at his glass as if it were a crystal ball
or piece of lathework, finished, done, no turning back.

We were at a rig just south of Tyrone, Oklahoma,
in No Man's Land one day inspecting thread damage
on some battered drill pipe when Roy suddenly
turned away and moved into the shadow of our truck,
head down, almost cowering, the dark wing of anguish
sweeping across his face. *It's the light*, he said.
*Fucking treeless Oklahoma. Strong light sometimes
brings it on.* He reached into the cab and handed me
some rubber tubing. *I'll stay here in the shade.
I'll be o.k. But if it comes, put this between my teeth
so I don't bite my tongue. Don't worry. I'll know ahead
of time. I'll warn you.* But of course there was no warning
this time as the sun broke behind a cloud and his body
dropped to earth thudding, writhing, shoveling dust
all around as his heels dug in, legs shaking, hands
clawing the ground, and his teeth gnashing so terribly
I could hardly wedge the rubber bar between them.
The St. Christopher was wound around his neck
so tight I had to break its chain, his eyes flaring

and rolling back white as cue balls when the gagging
began its dry sucking sound, that rattle and gasp,
and I knew then that it, the thing, had to be done:
Is there a more intimate gesture than placing one's hand
in the mouth of another man? All I could think
as I groped inside that mess of flesh and wetness
was how we would be seen from the rig's deck: two men,
one writhing in the dirt, the other strangling him
in the last throes of dying, and when it was over
and he lay there breathing fast and staring at the sky,
I thought that I had died, not him, and I rose up
and watched with dead eyes two dust devils in the distance
spinning out across the barren fields of No Man's Land.

The Journal: *Told Maria today. Says it's just too dangerous. But what*
the hell else can I do? Terrible, terrible sight for a young kid. This time
on a bridge with Maria, the river is black, sky black, a photographic
negative. That bizarre music again, like The Isle of the Dead. *The*
rising into light, probably only a second, but so slow. Nijinsky, now
there was a man with a fire in his head. <u>*And kingdoms naked in the*</u>
<u>*trembling heart—Te Deum laudamus O Thou Hand of Fire.*</u>

I know how Roy and I must look to you, she said.
We seem like . . . , she tried, *you must think . . .*
Roy passed out on phenobarbital, radio off,
we were driving back from Wichita where our team
had won a tournament that day. Grain elevator,
church spire in the distance, one more small town,
and twenty miles after that, another. A patch

of soybean flung forward by the sweep of headlights,
long shadow of a stand of maize, then nothing
but the night sky slipping like a sequined and slowly
unwinding bolt of black cloth across the Buick's hood,
the earth rolling beneath the rolling car so that,
a child might think, they would return in time and space
to the same point, same field of bending wheat,
DeKalb sign rattling on a fence post, wind sifting
through high grass, moaning on barbed wire—*my life*, I thought.
I knew what she was trying hard to say, and not
to say: failure. *That's how Roy and I must seem to you.*
No, I said, *not at all*. But she wouldn't hear of it,
and so began the litany of failure in America,
wind pushing the tears sideways across her face,
Bright beginnings, yes, I guess, but no grief here,
none. By God, we've made a life, and that's enough:
a life. Listen, Nijinsky went nuts. Bronislava,
a driven woman. All those big-shot émigrés
in Santa Monica trying to believe they were on
vacation in the south of France. What brought us here,
I don't understand. One thing happens. Then another.
We make do. We survive. It's just not that complex.
Oh yes it was. I was seventeen, and I knew.
It was vast, entangled, difficult, profound.
And as we rolled on through the deep sleep of small towns
strewn along the highway, the odd light of a house
like a single unshut eye somewhere on the edge,
the silence of the high plains huge yet imminent,
like the earth's held breath, I knew, it was not here.

That's what I mean, stud, Roy would say, *that's my point*
exactly. The held breath. As if we haven't quite
begun yet to exist. That coming into being
still going on. That final form just waiting,
the world waiting. And it's not just geography,
though that's part of it. Anderson had a sense of this
in Winesburg, *those tragic little lives bordering*
on something unknown, possible, huge—Dickinson,
too, sitting in her little room, Jesus, the walls
must have vibrated. For God's sake, this is not
the Wasteland, kid. London is. Or Paris.
This place has no history. And if you want to see
the absolute end of the road, try Venice.
You'll fall in love with her, everybody does,
but on the honeymoon you'll find you're crawling
in bed with a corpse. There are people still living
in this town who came up on the Jones and Plummer trail
when the only law was that the strong survived
and the weak didn't, who knew and lived something that
Kropotkin only dreamed: a state of total anarchy.
You know, L.A. was once like this. And then Chandler
and his pals moved in and conspired to do
what Lorenzo de' Medici had planned for Florence
and the Arno: divert a river so that one town
died and another prospered. So L.A. grew
and became what? A false Florence with faux-European
architecture, fake art (read Nathanael West),
synthetic landscape, and right next door on the coast,
a phony Venice with canals and everything.
And Chandler became the new, improved Medici,

all spiritual possibility gone, bought and sold,
infinities of human imagination
subdivided and air-conditioned. And, of course,
the new politics: metaphysical democracy—
nothing is genuine, everything is equally unreal.
Well, I'd rather be here.
                    And he pulled a book
from the shelf and read again in a too-loud,
prophetic voice those strange lines from Crane's *The Bridge*:

   And kingdoms
                naked in the
                        trembling heart—
   Te Deum laudamus
                O Thou Hand of Fire

So I've forgotten nothing, but if I had,
I would still remember this: one evening after
working late to finish out a load of drill pipe
when Maria drove up as usual to take us home
but made us wait in the car with the headlights on.
So we waited, high beams bright as stage lights against
the big front door in the midnight dark. We heard
the electric lift begin to hum as the door rose
slowly to reveal, inside, Maria in her white slip.
No music. Just wind pushing bunch grass against
a stack of cold roll and the rattle of a strip
of tin siding somewhere. And she began to dance.
Against a backdrop of iron and steel, looming hulks
of lathes and drill presses, tools scattered in the grease

and dirt, this still lithe, slim, small-boned creature
began to move silently, just the dry, eggshell
shuffle of her feet against the floor, began to glide,
leaping, spinning, rising, settling like a paper
tossed and floating in a breeze. I saw her then the way
young men must have seen Isadora Duncan once,
the first time. And I remember thinking, so this
is how it was, had been, for her on stage in Paris
or California when there was a future in her life.
The idling engine made the headlights shudder
so her body shimmered in a kind of silver foam,
and then turning quickly in a sweeping motion
into the center of the light, she stopped, froze,
head lifted in profile, wide-eyed, looking astonished
and a little fearful, a face that I had seen before,
and late that night I found it in my Gombrich's:
the orphan girl, by Delacroix. And I can tell you
that since that evening it's the face I've looked for
in every woman that I've known.

The Journal: *The holy disease without the holiness. Worse, without
the words. Ex-poet. The X poet. I swallowed my tongue years ago.
Bad joke. But I still pray—a bird, rising. Cendrars: "Mental prayer
is the aviary of God."*

                  *It all came apart
in L.A.*, she said, studying me through a wine glass
after Roy had gone to bed. *Roy fell in
somehow with Robert Rossen, the master craftsman*

of screenplays, first writer on Sierra Madre
before Huston took it over. But Rossen was
an ex-Red who at first refused to testify and then
used fronts and pseudonyms, the way they all did
those awful years the blacklist was in force.
They had collaborated on a script about
the Owens River deal: buying up the land
of unsuspecting farmers, posing as agents
of the reclamation project, then rigging up
a bond issue that would bring the water
not to L.A., as advertised, but to land purchased
by the city fathers downtown who thereby
made a ton, believe me. Biggest land scam
in this country's history since Manhattan island.
And no one complained because they all got fat
somewhere down the line as the water poured in
and land values soared. As Roy always said,
it's history's greatest lesson: <u>if enough people</u>
<u>commit a crime, it's not a crime anymore</u>.
And because Roy was not a Red, they put his name
on the manuscript. What a stupid thing to do.
Of course, the script found its way downtown, some strings
were pulled, pressure brought to bear, and suddenly
Roy had no career, especially since through the tie
with Rossen he was suspect anyway. Her voice
was frayed, tough, the wine glass empty, the ashtray full.
So the drinking started, then later, after Bakersfield,
the seizures, more drink, Tegretol, phenobarbital,
Dilantin, the whole mess. But that was years ago.

She made a kind of smile that wavered at the end.
Life's been simplified for us. It's simple now.
But of course she was talking to herself, not me.
And I was thinking, this is it, how lives go on,
this is how it happens, what I do not understand.

But then, this too, this too: when I drove her home
one night in early summer and we sat outside
with the pulse of cicadas washing over us in waves.
No talk. But I felt there was something between us.
Her profile blurred by a patchwork of shadows, eyes
stealing the light from the trailer's window. A woman
twenty years my senior. It wasn't sex. Not quite.
God knows, I ached to know a woman, wanted it
so bad I could have cried. In fact, I did. But this was,
well, not even love, more like wonderment. Erotic,
yes, but still, frozen, not to be acted on. She turned
to me *and knew what I knew* and smiled and went in,
or started to, then turned around, walked slowly back,
slid into the seat and still smiling looked at me
a long time before reaching over to place her hand
behind my head and carefully, delicately, as if
there were only a slight coolness moving there,
running the tip of her tongue along my lips.
Until it ended, the earth was breathing, it seemed,
or the space around us had become some sort
of immense beating heart, and when she peeled back
my shirt, and her lips—damp and unmercifully
soft—moved down my chest and belly, I believe

that I was actually trembling, a small wing beating
in my throat as she took me into her mouth
and afterwards placed her hand flat on my chest, just so,
as if to say, *a gift, just this once, never again.*

But this was before the summer dust and heat
came down the way it does in July heavy as sleep
so I felt half-drunk running the pipe rack, unloading
flat-bed haulers rumbling in each day, drivers sitting
on their fat asses letting me do all the work, and so
I mashed my foot between two drill collars and spent
the next few days in bed terribly happy reading
Flannery O'Connor and laughing myself well again.
Two or three weeks later, my father called me over.
Take a look. At his feet lay a sort of concrete bullet,
or bomb, sand-colored, with what seemed little flecks
of glass on the tapered part. *You know what that is?*
Well, that's the end of the story, bud. His foot nudged
the nose of the thing as if it were a dead deer.
The diamond bit. Chunks of low-grade diamond embedded
in the cutting surface. Can drill through anything.
So the old tri-cone's out. With this one they can stay
in the hole forever, and you know what that means.
And I did. Almost our whole business was threading pipe.
On oil rigs, pulling five thousand feet of drill pipe
in and out of the hole to change bits damaged
pipe joints. With the new bit, less damage, less work.
For us, a lot less. Not enough to make a profit.
Not even enough to pay costs. Amazing. And so,

it was all over, or soon would be. I looked at the face
of my father staring into the future, at the shop
he had built, the lathes lined up along the north side,
their iron song almost unbroken through twenty years,
the never-washed, grease-laden windows, gutted drawworks,
gears, bushings, tools spilled across the now scarred,
cement floor where I had worked every summer
since I was ten. And then a feather grazed my ear,
the ruffle of wings, and a vision rose in my head:
I was free. My future lay clear and open and bright
as the treeless field across the road. The burden
of inheritance now lifted, vanished. No shop.
Anything: musician, writer, anything I wanted.
I walked out into an endless sky. I rose. I flew.

The death of the shop was slow. Over the next year
or so work tapered off, as we knew it would,
and the welders and machinists walked away,
slowly, one by one. My father found other jobs
for them, in Midland, Snyder, towns like that,
and I put off college for a year to pick up the slack.
Roy and Maria dropped by the house on their way
out of town, Buick idling in the driveway, top down.
Come here, she said. She kissed my forehead, *Be good
to the girls, treat them right*. And Roy lit a cigar
and pointed to a box of books beside the car:
Read, learn a thing or two. They could have been going
to a wedding, all eager and bright, *nothing wrong here*,
and the car swaggered out, crunching gravel and squealing

onto Highway 54 with that Airstream trailer
gleaming in the distance, a silver sun floating
on heat waves along a straight black line of asphalt
to Route 66 and whatever would happen next.

Roy died a year later of a brain aneurism
at Maria's sister's house while he was watching
a Dodgers' game on TV. He always said
that when the Dodgers moved from Brooklyn to L.A.,
the world began to die. Well, I guess it did.
I came home from college for Christmas break
to find the Buick in our driveway. *Maria had it
driven here*, my father said. *After Roy died,
she didn't want it. She wanted you to have it.*
When he handed me the title, placed in my palm
that small, pink slip of paper with Maria's name
on it, it lay in my hand until my hand moved,
which was a long time.
    Along with it was a message
about the Buick's trunk, where I found a box
marked ROY'S STUFF, and inside Maria's note:

*It's not much, most of it from the Paris years, tip of the iceberg, really,
a lot written but a ton thrown away. After L.A., Roy could never
finish anything. I think he never wanted to see it take final form.
Always possible, but not quite there. You could say he fell in love with
the blank page, the about-to-be-written. You know his rules: pay atten-
tion, forget nothing, worship the imagination. And he followed them,
even if there's not much left to show.*

And then she gave her sister's address in L.A.
I looked the poems over, a mystery to me then,
though I've begun to see now, I believe, the ghosts
of Cendrars, Ponge, and Char standing over them.
And at the bottom of the box were pages photocopied
from a journal with this entry among the others:

*It goes on. It goes on and on. Tonight, after dinner. We danced.
The old music. We have nothing, really. Nothing but ourselves.*

That something may remain. When I returned from college
that next summer, the trucking business was picking up,
and my father and I began to think that we could turn
the shop to making custom truck beds. Make some money.
Stay afloat. Besides, college was such a disappointment.
Nobody read there. Well, maybe the professors,
in their "area of specialty," if that means anything.
Who could have known? There was a farm kid from Sublette
who said he came to learn Italian to read Dante
the way he should be read, but he transferred out.
I could write better, anyway, at home, I thought.
I was pretty lonely. But there were still the movies,
where I spent my extra time. When I drove there
one Friday night that winter, it had snowed, heavy,
about five inches, and I hadn't even bothered
to brush it off the car. The movie wasn't much,
but there was one scene I can't forget. A man,
a lonely small-town jeweler who is deaf and mute,
has that day lost his best friend, the friend he loves,

and as he walks the streets blind with grief, his hands
begin to move across his chest in sign language.
He is talking to himself. His hands move swiftly,
furiously, like small birds fighting in midair, then
faster, a blur, the mad flight of a man's hands
speaking hugely but silently, clamoring,
crying out, . . . and then it stops. The hands drop
to his sides. Without motion. Without speech.
A man walks down the street with his hands at his sides,
and so does everyone else. And who can tell
the difference?
                    Strange to think of all this now—
another time, another country, where I look down
each night on the lights of Paris littering the river—
but when I emerged from darkness into the coarse glare
of street lamps, it had warmed up, and walking toward
the car, I could see the snow melting and dropping off,
small pieces sliding off the hood and down the fenders,
the big Buick rising from the snow with patches
of watery blue emerging as it rose. I stopped
ten feet or so away and stared at it, astonished,
stunned, *that coming into being still going on*,
as the white top snow-laden beneath the street lamp
gave off rainbow colors, iridescent, the hard fire
of a thousand jewels, and wherever on the metal
the snow had melted was the glazed blue, looking
brilliant, deeper, bluer than it had ever been.
I stood there a long time listening to the soft crush
of clumps of snow as they dropped onto the street and then,

in the background, hearing the night sounds of horns
far away and a lone shout somewhere close by
and watching the lights in the gleaming blue surface
from passing cars and from the stars and the moon
and from anywhere there was any light at all
as all things seen and unseen and all kingdoms
naked in the human heart rose toward the sky.

Three Poems by Roy Eldridge Garcia

Mlle Pym

On Saturday Mlle Pym would marry a philatelist, and her relatives had decided to boycott the wedding. They were as tolerant as the next person, but since the death of Uncle Max, an assistant postmaster, stamps had been banished from the family. Uncle Max was a funny man, full of laughter and clever banter, and even a single stamp resting in one's palm seemed cruelly to point to his absence, his wit that had brightened the house for some fifty years. However, Mlle Pym, who loathed Uncle Max's stale jokes, felt no qualms about yielding to the philatelist's advances, awkward as they were. The announcement of their wedding was sent by special delivery. Each wedding invitation carried ten five-centime stamps, each of a different color. So when the couple found only strangers at the wedding, they were angered but not surprised. The ceremony was flawless, and emerging from the church, the bride and her philatelist were showered with stamps from all countries, of every hue and shape. There was Portugal, green with rose edging, and quaint Bolivia, imperial in its bold blue. And fluttering ominously down to rest in the bride's outstretched hand was Iceland, pale and triangular, damp from the tongue of a stranger.

The Levitations

On the second night of the levitations, he saw Maria hovering above St. Eustache and began to fear that she would never return. At first the fear was only a twinge, a doubt, at the base of his brain, but soon it grew to a moan, then a mélange of several voices, and finally a chorus of sighs so heavy, so massive, that he prayed that he, too, would rise. But his feet were fixed to the ground, and tears rolled down his face in great dollops of gold and silver. Even from such a distance, positioned above one of the raging gargoyles, Maria was able to reassure him, *It's only a kind of mind storm, the clouds of Ulro, the bad weather of the turning soul, and you need not to pray but to wake up. Wake up*, she whispered, *wake up*. Her voice drifted ever so lightly down to him, swirled around him, embraced him, and he felt himself rising toward her, with the shops, the stone streets glittering in rain, M. Yousif's little café where he smoked his first hashish, the chestnut trees in their wire skirts, the *boule* courts where he whiled away the hours after work, the bookstalls, all the things he loved but never knew he loved, receding as he rose. But when he looked to the south, the great river was ablaze, and the souls of the damned cried out in terror and indescribable suffering, and falling now, slowly, like a leaf floating in the late autumn air, he knew of course that he would never, never wake.

A Man in a Machine Shop

after René Char

A man went into a machine shop to look for something and in the process of looking for it forgot what it was. Lingering among shadows, he mused upon this strange country of forgetfulness and the journey that had brought him there. For a while he had belonged to something, had placed himself at its service, and now it had passed over the horizon leaving not a trace behind. However, he took some comfort in the shadows. Their depths and contours seemed to hold a promise, a wistful silence that drew him farther and farther into the darkness of the shop. "How remarkable," he thought, "to be thus cast into a strange country and to find myself so soon in the company of friends." For there was a nostalgia in the darkness, a gentle returning like the voices of those he had known before he came to the country of forgetfulness. Sinking deeper into a corner of the shop, he knelt next to a broken pump and touched his forehead to his knees. The shadows now moved over him like an enormous quilt, quite pleasant at first, but then covering him with such an oppressive warmth that he found himself weeping and twitching his ears as he had done at the barbershop as a child. The country began to crawl beneath him like an escalator, and as he gave himself to its unalterable descent, he heard the far roar of an ocean and the cry of gulls and soon felt the undertow of memory clutching at his feet.

PART FOUR

A Wall Map of Paris

. . . tragend als Strömung das Haupt und die Leier.
Rilke

A night of drinking, dawn is coming on,
my friend's hand falls along a darkening stain
that runs from Vaugirard to Palatine
and west to Rue Cassette. *There*, he says,
*Rilke wrote "The Panther." And that darkness
came from James Wright's head one soggy night
when he drank too much, leaned back into the Seine,
and recited verse till dawn.* Ohio sunlight
stuns the windowpane, and I'm seeing Paris,
where the morning bronzes cobblestones,
the grates around the chestnut trees, and a man
with a fullback's shoulders and a dancer's tread
whistles a Schubert tune and walks toward
a river like the rivers in his head.

He looks for Villon's ghost at Notre Dame,
recalls Apollinaire, the rain-soaked heart
of sad Verlaine, Rilke at the Dome,
and later at St. Anne's watches children
learning how to kiss like swans. But on
Pont Neuf, when he gazes deep into the Seine,
the face of a glassworker's son stares back,
and the river that runs through Paris runs

through Ohio past Jimmy Leonard's shack,
the Shreve High Football Stadium, and Kenyon,
where a boy with the memory of a god
and a gift for taking images to heart
translates from a poem about the head
of Orpheus, in a river, singing.

A Photograph of the *Titanic*

When Travis came home from the monastery,
the ground had vanished beneath him,
and he went everywhere in bare feet

as if he were walking on a plane of light,
and he spoke of his sleepless nights
and of a picture in *National Geographic*:

a pair of shoes from the *Titanic* resting
on the ocean floor. They were blue
against a blue ground and a black garden

of iron and brass. The toes pointed outward,
toward two continents, and what had been
inside them had vanished so completely

that he imagined it still there, with the sea's
undersway bellying down each night
as each day after compline he fell into

his bed, the dark invisible bulk of tons
pushing down on the shoes, nudging them
across the blue floor, tossing them aside

like a child's hands in feverish sleep
until the shoestrings scattered and dissolved.
Sometimes he would dream of the shoes

coming to rest where it is darkest,
after the long fall before we are born,
when we gather our bodies around us,

when we curl into ourselves and drift
toward the little sleep we have rehearsed
again and again as if falling we might drown.

The Deposition

And one without a name
Lay clean and naked there, and gave commandments.
Rilke, "Washing the Corpse" (trans. Jarrell)

Dust storm, we thought, a brown swarm
plugging the lungs, or a locust-cloud,
but this was a collapse, a slow sinking
to deeper brown, and deeper still, like the sky
seen from inside a well as we are lowered down,
and the air twisting and tearing at itself.

But it was done. And the body hung there
like a butchered thing, naked and alone
in a sudden hush among the ravaged air.
The ankles first—slender, blood-caked,
pale in the sullen dark, legs broken
below the knees, blue bruises smoldering
to black. And the spikes. We tugged iron
from human flesh that dangled like limbs
not fully hacked from trees, nudged
the cross beam from side to side until
the sign that mocked him broke loose.
It took all three of us. We shouldered the body
to the ground, yanked nails from wrists
more delicate, it seemed, than a young girl's
but now swollen, gnarled, black as burnt twigs.

The body, so heavy for such a small man,
was a knot of muscle, a batch of cuts
and scratches from the scourging, and down
the right side a clotted line of blood,
the sour posca clogging his ragged beard,
the eyes exploded to a stare that shot
through all of us and still speaks in my dreams:
I know who you are.

                So, we began to wash
the body, wrenching the arms, now stiff
and twisted, to his sides, unbending
the ruined legs and sponging off the dirt
of the city, sweat, urine, shit—all the body
gives—from the body, laying it out straight
on a sheet of linen rank with perfumes
so that we could cradle it, haul it
to the tomb. The wind shouted.
The foul air thickened. I reached over
to close the eyes. *I know who you are.*

A Starlit Night

All over America at this hour men are standing
by an open closet door, slacks slung over one arm,
staring at wire hangers, thinking of taxes
or a broken faucet or their first sex: the smell
of back-seat Naugahyde, the hush of a maize field
like breathing, the stars rushing, rushing away.

And a woman lies in an unmade bed watching
the man she has known twenty-one, no,
could it be? twenty-two years, and she is listening
to the polonaise climbing up through radio static
from the kitchen where dishes are piled
and the linoleum floor is a great, gray sea.

It's the A-flat polonaise she practiced endlessly,
never quite getting it right, though her father,
calling from the darkened TV room, always said,
"Beautiful, kiddo!" and the moon would slide across
the lacquered piano top as if it were something
that lived underwater, something from far below.

They both came from houses with photographs,
the smell of camphor in closets, board games
with missing pieces, sunburst clocks in the kitchen
that made them, each morning, a little sad.
They didn't know what they wanted, every night,
every starlit night of their lives, and now they have it.

Motion Sickness

I am tired of the heave and swell,
the deep lunge in the belly, the gut's
dumb show of dance and counterdance,
sway and pause, the pure jig of nausea
in the pit of a spinning world.
Where the body moves, the mind
often lags, clutching deck, anchor,
the gray strap that hangs like the beard
of death from the train's ceiling,
the mind lost in the slow bulge
of ocean under the moon's long pull
or the endless coil of some medieval
argument for the existence of God
or the dream of the giant maze
that turns constantly in and in
on itself and there is no way out . . .
I am sick and tired of every rise and fall
of the sun, the moon's tedious cycle
that sucks blood from the thighs of women
and turns teenage boys into wolves
prowling the streets, hungry for motion.
Let me be still, let me rest
in some hollow of space and time
far from the seasons and that boring,
ponderous drama of day and night.
Let me sleep in the heart of calm

and dream placidly of birds frozen
in the unmoving air of eternity
and the earth grown immobile
in its centrifugal spin, and God
motionless as Lazarus in his tomb
before he is raised dizzily
to fall again, to rise, to fall.

At the Café de Flore

This evening, as I am entering the Café de Flore to buy some cigarettes, I meet Levastine with a half-drunken companion who introduced himself as the "abbé défroque surréaliste." He was the first surrealist priest.

Mircea Eliade, Journal I, 1945–1955

I have anointed boutonnieres and cats,
preached homilies on spectacles and bats,
baptized the morning, evening, and full moon,
and blessed both happiness and gloom.
I proclaim the doctrine of broken clocks:
on every hour, remove your shoes and socks,
sing the Marseillaise nine times backwards
and consider, please, the lives of birds
(there are fewer than before the war).
Père Surréaliste does not wish to bore
with his prayers to orchids and champagne,
the sanctity of wine, the uselessness of pain,
but twenty miles from here are flowers
growing from the mouths of boys.
For what I've seen there is no word,
I am the Priest of the Absurd.

At Omaha Beach

Lewis M. Ginsberg
d. June 7, 1944

The waves wash out, wash in.
The rain comes down. It comes down.
The sky runs into the sea
that turns in its troubled sleep,
dreaming its long gray dream.
White stars stand on the lawn.
We move on the edges of speech.

Sleep comes down. It comes down.
Dreams wash out, wash in.
Our fathers walk out of the sea.
The air is heavy with speech.
Our fathers are younger than we.
As the fog dissolves in the dawn,
our fathers lie down on the beach.

We're a dream drifting down on a beach
in the rain in the sleep of our lives.
White stars wash over a lawn.
We are troubled by sea and sky.
Our words dissolve in the waves.
On the edges of speech is the sound
of the rain coming down. It comes down.

W. Y. Evans-Wentz, Keystone Hotel, San Diego

> *But in Tolstoy, just as in Plato and Plotinus, the thought of*
> *death is accompanied by a particular sentiment, by a kind*
> *of consciousness that, even while horror rose before them, wings*
> *were growing in their backs.*
>
> Lev Shestov, "A Letter to His Daughters"

Evans-Wentz is dying as he rises
into San Diego's morning, waking
to admire the yellow kitchen gathering
the light, postcards of saints above the stove,
and the smiling bodhisattva by the door.
He makes a simple breakfast, dresses, leaves,
greets the hotel clerk and doorman—drowsy
in their heavy bodies, dark in the mystery
of their hidden lives—then pauses on
the sidewalk below the orange Rexall sign
where the slanting light opens like a door
to all the light-filled mornings of his life
and then slams shut with the blare and wail
of car horns, screeching truck tires braking
for the crowds. Looking up, he crosses slowly,
leaning on his carved, Tibetan cane,
to the public library where Miss Thorpe keeps
his books behind the desk and waits for him.
He takes one down, *The Tibetan Book*
of the Dead, translated by one Evans-Wentz,
reads again the *Bardo*, the passage of the soul

to rebirth after death, then thinks of sunlight,
the blazing, traffic-haunted street he crossed,
the Santa Ana river that he swam in
as a boy, his body half-in, half-out
of water, the way the sun would shed itself
in copper leaves floating at his fingertips
and those leaves told him what his life would be.
When he shuts the book at noon, Miss Thorpe
smiles to see him cross the street and stand again
below the orange sign, his arms spread wide
in a shaft of light: Evans-Wentz is dying.

The Problem

The name of the bow is life, but its work is death.
The Fragments

How in Heraclitus
ideas of things, quality, and event
coalesce—sun/warmth/dawn—
the perceiver/perceived, too,
not yet parsed, not yet,
and then the great Forgetting,
breath and breather, love and beloved,
world and God-in-the-world.

But then it comes upon us: that brightness,
that bright tension in animals, for instance,
that focus, that compass
of the mammalian mind finding
its own true North,
saintly in its dark-eyed,
arrow-eared devotion.
A kind of calling, a *via negativa*,
a surrender, still and silent, to the heart's desire.

So in the cathedral of the world
we hold communion,
the bread of language
placed delicately upon our tongues

as we breathe the bitter air,

drinking the wine of reason

and pressing to our breasts the old dream of Being.

Two Scenes

I. WHITE HORSE IN RAIN

It could be a dream dissolving
as the rain grows heavier,
the pale horse of the apocalypse
come to put an end to weather.

A darkness of hemlock and white pine
surrounds the meadow, and the flies
that rapped like blind men on the panes
are gone. Behind the rain's gray gauze

a whiteness moves, slow, meandering—
a light in fog, a face behind a grate,
a shout receding down a street
where all dreams end: a life, a fate.

II. WHITE HORSE IN SUNLIGHT

One might consider the way
at death the metaphors narrow—
sleep, rest, passing on, leaving—
like light focused through a glass
to a blue-white point,
a brilliant literalness.

Along the tree line
the blood leaves of red oak
deepen because the horse is white,
its head lowered to earth, and the figure
that comes to mind is prayer,
but also desire, the lover and beloved,
the grass on fire.

The white horse in sunlight,
neither desire nor death.
The ghost horse of *dasein*,
the white flame of *to be*,
the world a broad, vague pasture
where a horse stands in the weight
and locus of its centrality.

PART FIVE

The Memory Palace

The next stage is memory, which is like a great field or a spacious palace. . . . It is a vast, immeasurable sanctuary. Who can plumb its depths? And yet it is a faculty of my soul. Although it is part of my nature, I cannot understand all that I am. This means, then, that the mind is too narrow to contain itself entirely. But where is that part of it which it does not itself contain? Is it somewhere outside itself and not within it? How, then, can it be a part of it, if it is not contained in it?

St. Augustine, *Confessions*

He inferred that persons desiring to train this faculty (of memory) must select places and form mental images of the things they wish to remember and store those images in the places, so that the order of the places will preserve the order of the things, and the images of the things will denote the things themselves, . . .

Cicero in *De oratore*, speaking of the poet Simonides

It is dark but will soon be light. We will place them here, in each room, on each machine, each part your hands touched repeatedly, all those surfaces glossed now with moonlight raining through the slats in the roof.

There is a certain urgency about this, like the undertow at Galveston when you almost drowned. A certain pull.

It is the machine shop, of course, because you saw your father build it and your mother worry over it and both of them quarrel and grieve over it, and you worked there, and it became the air your family breathed, the food they ate. It is all around you and inside you, and for reasons you cannot know, it contains everything you did or felt or thought.

There is, first, your version of paradise, Avenue "J" in Houston, your father just back from the war, a working-class neighborhood before television pulled everyone inside, all the fathers home from work, mothers calling from front porches, and all your people— Bert, Locie, your sister, Marie, your aunt and uncle—sitting on blankets in the backyard, the good talk and laughter in the darkening air, and to commemorate this, along with the things of your life, we place throughout the shop, draped across the backs of lathes and drill presses and milling machines, the sentences you never want to forget, sentences from the first prose you ever read that made the word, *beauty*, form in your mind and made you want to write, to write sentences.

On the rough wet grass of the backyard my father and mother have spread quilts. We all lie there, my mother, my father, my uncle, my aunt, and I too am lying there.

Out back in the welding shop where men were gods, Vulcans in black helmets, and the blaze of cutting torches hurled onto the ceiling the gigantic shadows you watched as a child, place here the things of gods and children: baseball; a twilight double-header and the blue bowl of the sky as the lights came on; the fragrance of mown grass in the outfield; the story about the great pitcher, Moses Yellowhorse; your first double play at second base, the feeling of having your body disappear inside a motion; O. T. Swearingen holding his infant grandson in the shadow of the door of the great barn where it was always night; the storm cellar, the great yawn of the door, and then the going down, the rank earth smells, the swallowing up.

In the center, next to the grinder, place the image of your grandmother, her legs ribbed with varicose veins. O.T., haunted by night terrors, would call out in his sleep, *Nellie, Nellie.* In the morning in the kitchen with the slanted floor, you would stare at her legs, the purple cords, and think, she has walked so far in this kitchen, has walked to another country, and O.T. was calling her back.

First we were sitting up, then one of us lay down, and then we all lay down, on our stomachs, or on our sides, or on our backs, and they have kept on talking.

In the tool-and-die shed that has no windows, things seen in half-light, dimly remembered, almost—but not quite—understood: the woman who scavenged trash cans late at night wearing a high school formal, walking the alleys, the tin clutter of her life rattling through the town; standing in line at the supermarket yesterday, there it was in your head, the hum of the lathe, song of the honing cloth, a child's song heard from a distance; shooting hoops after sunset, the whisper of the net in the darkness; and, oh yes, that summer night after the drive-in, something silky hanging from the rearview mirror of the blue Buick, the Gioconda smile on Dee Dee Loeffler's face.

They are not talking much, and the talk is quiet, of nothing in particular, of nothing at all in particular, of nothing at all.

King Lear performed on the bank of the Trinity River in Fort Worth. Early evening, chorus of cicadas behind you, Lear in agony, played badly. The eyes of your son and daughter bright with stage light. You have no words for bliss and so lose yourself in the stars. On the way home, everyone sings, *If You've Got the Money, Honey, I've Got the Time.* Drape this over the lathe your father worked, days and sometimes nights, for twenty-seven years.

The stars are wide and alive, they seem each like a smile of great sweetness, and they seem very near.

Over here, in the lap of the big drill press, where the drill froze and you panicked, place all things sudden: Uncle Harry breaking into a Fred Astaire soft-shoe; waking in Kansas to snowfall—the hush, the heart's cathedral, the last echoes of the choir floating down, your breath fogging the window, bleaching the trees; the great dust storm, crawling home on your hands and knees so you could feel the sidewalk; old Mrs. Pate's elm clogged with grackles, then bursting in a chattering black cloud of feathers and falling leaves.

All my people are larger bodies than mine, quiet, with voices gentle and meaningless like the voices of sleeping birds.

The field on the west is dressed out with tropes: Keats's untrodden region of the mind, Dickinson's cathedral tunes, Donne's compass, Jarrell's "waist the spirit breaks its arm on," all the ones in Plath's "Medallion." Nearest, just opposite the big pipe straightener, will be the first ones, from the Old Testament, invisible to fundamentalists. And you will always need them because you hunger always for things seen in the light of everything else, and the light is endless.

The strangest event in your life, your baptism, because you walked through a doorway but arrived in the same room: place it here, in the office where the elderly bookkeeper, Mr. Mayfield, kept meticulous records. An inventory. And your mother weeping because your life was saved, rescued, like Jimmy Deeds pulled from the river, still breathing. Saved, accounted for.

One is my mother who is good to me. One is my father who is good to me.

On the faceplate of the milling machine, where iron filings spilled into a child's outstretched hands, place things felt, the biography of your skin: falling off to sleep, the cool palms of the sheets, the lightness of your body; your first French kiss, your hand on the small breasts of Samantha Dobbins, her belly, her thigh, the astonishing softness, her quickening breath in the shallow of your neck; waves lapping your ankles like little mouths; the pugil stick in your stomach, the blacking out; the nail in the foot; the car wreck when you were four, touching your mother's face, the tiny slivers of glass flickering red and blue in the police car's lights.

On the top shelf of this iron cabinet, circling the toolbox, the ornaments of labor: the time card, punched, with eight hours remaining; *The Machinist's Handbook*; the metal hard hat with the leather liner smelling of thirty years of sweat; the aluminum black lunch box with the Captain Marvel decal, the copy of Fitzgerald's *Odyssey* inside; the steel burr they removed from your father's eye, work gloves lying in the gathering bin, where he threw them.

By some chance, here they are, all on this earth . . . lying, on quilts, on the grass, in a summer evening, among the sounds of the night.

Along the bedways of the small lathe, where the long window gathered the afternoon light and you could feel the last layers of the workday falling away, place these: an orange grove in California, 1944, the song-like, soprano voices of women lifting and falling; your first library book, *Biography of a Grizzly*, read on the corner of 3rd and Kansas, the traffic of the world suddenly frozen around you; the high school photo of Patricia Lea Gillespie, a little frightened, the future coming on too fast, too fast; a small boy in a T-shirt that says, I'D RATHER BE IN PHILADELPHIA; a girl with her hair in a bun, dancing for her aunts and uncles, who have promised to cover their eyes; your old friend Radke's painting, *The Arrival of the Future*, the future a halo of wasps around his head; your uncle Bill Branum, the funniest man you ever knew, dying of lung cancer, hand dropping onto a steel tray, cigarette ash floating across a white tile floor; the beach at Galveston at sunset, lavender glass and chrome of the waves flattening out, the last light dragged out to sea, darkening sand, voices of your kinfolk lifting gull-like, that flight of laughter, twilight glimmer of beer cans, a black dog, cigarettes, faces squinting at the sun; the sun.

May God bless my people, my uncle, my aunt, my mother, my good father, oh, remember them kindly in their time of trouble; and in the hour of their taking away.

And this: the day during a viral fever you felt your Self detaching itself and moving like a boat unmoored from a dock slowly but irretrievably away from your body, and the terror was more real than your body. Do not forget this, for it was Hell. Hang this from the hook of the center hoist.

And this, on the iron beam where the sparrows gathered: St. Joseph's Hospital, and through the big window you watched two birds in the distance, two white flames swooping in great, crossing arcs against the leaves of date palms, and you concentrated hard on that until the pain in your lungs fell away, diminished until it seemed very distant, hardly there at all. You were astonished at the beauty of the birds. This is grace, you thought. No, this is *grace on fire*.

After a little I am taken in and put to bed.

And this: in the backyard of the little white rent-house with the Spanish moss hanging down, tossing a Frisbee to your son, and when his small body curved up and out to catch it, a beam of light broke over the corner of the house and passed between his fingertips and the orange disk, and time froze, and three hundred years later he came down and you rose to get another beer from the refrigerator.

All of this, and more, you must hang onto, you must, but time is running out, here is your daughter on stage, a goddess, the beauty of it is overwhelming; your son rounding the bases the first time, grinning; your wife, oh this one, with her face veiled in half-shadow, the eyes weary, a life written across her forehead, her hand touching your wrist, that touch, that evening.

Sleep, soft smiling, draws me unto her: and those receive me, who quietly treat me, as one familiar and well-beloved in that home: but will not, oh, will not, not now, not ever; but will not ever tell me who I am.

Look around, see how they are all positioned, each in its place. Now you can remember everything. But there's no more time, it's morning, time to go to work, and they are opening the huge shop door, that slow rumble you will never forget, and the light leaking in, widening—light like a quilt of gold foil flung out so it will drape all of this, will keep it and keep it well—and it is so bright now, you can hardly bear it as it fills the door, this immense glacier of light coming on, and still you do not know who you are, but here it is, try to remember, it is all beginning:

NOTES

"Moses Yellowhorse Is Throwing Water Balloons from the Hotel Roosevelt": Moses Yellowhorse played one and a half seasons for the Pittsburgh Pirates, 1921–1922, always listed on the roster as Chief Yellowhorse. The famous game in which he struck out Gehrig, Ruth, and Lazzeri in succession occurred during spring training.

"Holy Rollers, Snyder, Texas, 1951": No Man's Land, which also appears in "History" and "The Blue Buick: A Narrative," was a standard designation for that portion of the Oklahoma Panhandle which was effectively without state or federal legal authority or powers of enforcement until the late nineteenth century and thus became a convenient refuge for criminals, real or alleged, from other parts of the country.

"The Welder, Visited by the Angel of Mercy": Because the present book in various ways grew out of this poem, I have reprinted it from *The Art of the Lathe* (Farmington, Maine: Alice James Books, 1998), pp. 70–71.

"The Blue Buick: A Narrative": The Cendrars epigraph is my translation from the Folio reprint of the 1949 Denoël edition of *Le Lotissement du ciel (The Subdividing of the Sky)*, edited and annotated by Claude Leroy, pp. 406–407:

> . . . je lisais les Classiques dans une édition anglaise; mais il m'arrivait aussi, toujours pour me distraire, de dérouler une carte du ciel sur la grande table et de recouvrir chaque constellation avec des pierres précieuses que j'allais quérir dans la réserve des coffres, marquant les étoiles de premiere grandeur avec les plus beaux diamants, complétant les figures avec les plus vivantes pierres de couleur remplissant les intervalles entre les dessins avec une coulee des plus belles perles de la collection de Léouba, . . . Elles étaient toutes belles! Et je me récitais la page immortelle et pour moi inoubliable de Marbode sur la symbolique des pierres précieuses que je venais de découvrir dans *Le*

Latin mystique de Rémy de Gourmont, ce livre gemmé, une compilation, une traduction, un anthologie, qui a bouleversé ma conscience et m'a, en somme, baptisé ou, tout au moins, converti à la Poésie, initié au Verbe, catéchisé.

In his notes, Leroy quotes Cendrars in *Bourlinguer*: *"Le Latin mystique* a été pour moi une date, une date de naissance intellectuelle." In his journal, Roy's first quote from the section of *Sky* entitled *Le ravissement d'amour* is his translation of "Le saint aussi a ses migraines et ses dégoûts de lassitude. . . . Il se méfie de l'illusion, du somnambulisme comme dans les rêves, des acrobaties comme chez certains intoxiques et des attaques du haut mal, et des crises de nerfs comme chez certains épileptiques et névropathes" (p. 247). Roy's second quotation is also from that section: "L'oraison mentale est la volière de Dieu" (p. 244).

Roy's critique of Los Angeles refers to the construction of the Los Angeles Aqueduct, which, through "false droughts and artful title transactions" and the passing of a bond issue in 1905, diverted Owens River water from the Owens Valley and its farms and small towns and brought it two hundred and thirty-five miles southwest to the San Fernando Valley, where Chandler and other members of two land syndicates had recently "bought or optioned virtually the entire valley." As Joan Didion further notes in *After Henry* (New York: Vintage, 1992), pp. 222–223:

> The extent to which Los Angeles was literally invented by the *Los Angeles Times* and by its owners, Harrison Gray Otis and his descendants in the Chandler family, remains hard for people in less recent parts of the country to fully apprehend. At the time Harrison Gray Otis bought his paper there were only five thousand people living in Los Angeles. There was no navigable river. . . . Los Angeles has water today because Harrison Gray Otis and his son-in-law Harry Chandler wanted it, and fought a series of outright water wars to get it.

"A Wall Map of Paris": The epigraph is from Sonnet XXVI in the Second Part of *The Sonnets to Orpheus* (New York: Modern Library, 1995), translated by Stephen Mitchell, pp. 512–513. Mitchell's translation of the entire passage is

          —Oh compose the criers,
harmonious god! let them wake resounding,
let their clear stream carry the head and the lyre.

"The Problem": The epigraph is taken from the Oxford University Press
1959 edition of *Heraclitus*, translated and edited by Philip Wheelwright.
I am also indebted to Wheelwright's introduction and to comments on
Parmenides and on Stephen MacKenna's famous translation of Plotinus
which were given in a lecture by Donald Sheehan at the Frost Place,
Franconia, New Hampshire, in August 2001.